SHARING KNOWLEDGE AND EXPERIENCE

SHARING KNOWLEDGE AND EXPERIENCE

A Profile of
KWABENA NKETIA
Scholar and Music Educator

E. A. AKROFI

AFRAM PUBLICATIONS (GHANA) LIMITED

Published by:
Afram Publications (Ghana) Ltd.,
P.O. Box M 18,
Accra, Ghana

© **Eric Ayisi Akrofi,** 2002

All rights reserved. Except for use in any review, the reproduction or utilization of this work in whole or part in any form by any electronic, mechanical or other means, now known or hereafter invented, including xerography, photocopying and recording or in any information storage or retrieval system, is forbidden without the prior permission of the publishers, Afram Publications (Ghana) Limited.

First Published, 2002

ISBN: 9964 70 342 2

Printed by: Compuprint Ltd. Tel: 226942/230356

TABLE OF CONTENTS

ACKNOWLEDGEMENTS .... *ii*

FOREWORD .... *vi*

PREFACE .... *viii*

CHAPTER ONE
*MUSICAL EDUCATION AND THE FORMATIVE
PERIOD OF HIS LIFE* *1*

CHAPTER TWO
NKETIA AND HIS FAMILY *17*

CHAPTER THREE
THE LEGON YEARS 1952-1979 .... *25*

CHAPTER FOUR
THE AMERICAN YEARS 1979-1992 .... *47*

CHAPTER FIVE
*NKETIA'S RETURN TO GHANA:
A PERIOD OF REFLECTION* *58*

CHAPTER SIX
*THE EDUCATIONAL VALUE OF NKETIA'S
SOURCE MATERIALS* *69*

CHAPTER SEVEN
NKETIA'S THOUGHTS ON MUSIC EDUCATION *147*

CHAPTER EIGHT
*PRACTICAL APPLICATION OF ETHNOMUSICOLOGY
AND COMPOSITION IN THE PEDAGOGICAL PIECES
AND EXERCISES IN AFRICAN RHYTHM* *170*

CHAPTER NINE
NKETIA'S LEGACY *189*

NOTES *193*

BIBLIOGRAPHY *196*

APPENDIX
MUSICAL SCORES *203*

ACKNOWLEDGEMENTS

I am very grateful to Professor Kwabena Nketia for giving me full support for this study, and helping me sort out the title and the headings of the three chapters in part two of this work. I owe the photographs reproduced here to Dr. Akosua Perbi, Nketia's daughter and eldest child, who also provided most of the information in the second chapter of this study. Thanks are due to Professor Kofi Agawu for reading the manuscript and offering suggestions. I am indebted to Professor Akin Euba for providing me with relevant papers and music scores of some of Nketia's compositions. I also thank C.K. Adom for sending me some of the source materials of Nketia which are out-of-print and for providing me with up-to-date information on the activities of the latter. To Patrick Ofori, Librarian, University of Transkei, I owe another round of thanks for helping me to select a suitable title for this study prior to my acceptance of Nketia's proposed title; and for encouraging me to work steadily on this project. I am also indebted to Nomsa Nqolase, inter-library loans assistant, University of Transkei, for obtaining numerous publications of Nketia for me. Last, but not the least, I thank Thobeka Mqamelo for painstakingly typing the manuscript of this study.

Umtata, South Africa
November 2001

FOREWORD

AN AFRICAN VOICE IN MUSICOLOGY

Professor J. H. Kwabena Nketia Saben, Asona ba, renowned scholar, linguist, composer, poet, researcher, teacher and distinguished musicologist has made an imprint on African musicology. This occasion of his eighty first birthday is perhaps the most appropriate to bring together his rich, multifaceted and multidisciplinary career. I therefore consider it a special honour to have been called upon to write a foreword to this epoch-making text.

Professor Nketia's areas of activities can be viewed from three different perspectives: creative writing, teaching and scholarship, all of which are linked by a common thread derived from his early childhood and his acquired formal educational experiences in later life.

As a creative person Professor Nketia's activities cover the literary and the performing arts. His works include descriptive, narrative, fiction, poems and plays written in Twi, his mother tongue. He has remained an active collector, having edited annotated texts, traditional songs, and translated scientific booklets in Twi. As a composer, Professor Nketia has produced vocal works, instrumental ensembles, songs and solo pieces for piano.

As teacher, Professor Nketia taught Twi and music at

the Presbyterian Training College at Akropong in Ghana. At the University of Ghana, Legon, he taught music at the School of Music, Dance and Drama, within the Institute of African Studies of which he was the Director. This school was to provide a 'model' for the establishment of music departments in other African countries where music competes less favourably with other disciplines in tertiary institutions. He has also taught African music in other universities in different parts of Africa, United States, United Kingdom, and Europe and has delivered lectures on different aspects of African music in many institutions all over the world. Although his teaching career and general horizon are broad and transcend ethnic, national, and racial boundaries, his keen interest in African and Afro-American concerns is always discernible because of their shared cultural past. He encouraged Africans and Blacks in the Diaspora to engage in intensive research and documentation of their cultural traditions for urgent rediscovery of materials from the oral tradition and for a reassessment of existing theories on African music.

As a scholar, Professor Nketia bases his writings on materials collected from intensive fieldwork conducted among his own people in Ghana and in other parts of Africa. He has tackled fundamental issues such as the theoretical framework of African music, educational research and publications representing his own musical culture. His writings have, therefore, become standard references on issues germane to African musicology.

His own person epitomizes the picture of an Akan musician in the contemporary world; one who is thoroughly embedded in his own musical tradition as a base for his acquired education in Western musical traditions to produce an African identity. His educational experiences-both informal and formal- have enabled him to maintain a strong footing in his tradition which essentially has been responsible for his multidisciplinary approach to scholarship.

How can one assess the impact of the contributions of this great African scholar? We leave it to time and future generations. For the present, we can say that Professor Nketia is the pioneer of African musicology, in both theory and practice. He made the consciousness of African identity in music a reality and an imperative. He has promoted it in his professional life by works and by empowering Africans, Africans in the Diaspora as well as non-Africans to follow his path through the training programmes. This way he has been able to develop the 'African voice' in African musicology. During the years before him, the study of African music was in the hands of 'foreigners', the so-called 'outsiders' to the tradition. Through his efforts African musicology has now come to occupy its rightful place in the international world of music.

Indeed, Nketia's whole career as an African musicologist and his vision for the future of African musicology are epitomised by the International Centre for African Music and Dance (ICAMD) located at the University of

Ghana, Legon, with branches in different parts of Anglophone and Francophone Africa, and the United States of America. We rejoice with and celebrate you.

Kwabena Nketia Saben,
Asona ne Aduana ba
Wofiri Mampɔn Kontonkyi
Daammerɛ ɔboɔ hi Akuma
Waabɔ wo bra ama no asɔ tete nananom ani
Woako adi nkunim
Ma wo kanea nso ahyerɛn.

PROF. MOSUNMOLA OMIBIYI-OBIDIKE
Acting Director, Institute of African Studies,
University of Ibadan

PREFACE

Although I had known Professor J.H. Kwabena Nketia since I was a secondary school boy in the 1960s, I started getting interested in doing a serious study of his life and work when the editor of the International Journal of Music Education (IJME), Dr. Anthony E. Kemp, invited me in 1991 to write an article on the contributions of Professor Nketia to music education for the journal's "Personalities in World Music Education" series.

After the publication of my four-page article "Personalities in World Music Education No.14, J.H. Kwabena Nketia", (see IJME (19) 1992:41-45) devoted to Nketia's educational background, his career as a composer, and his work as a scholar, I was poised to do a more extensive biographical study of this outstanding musicologist, music educator, composer, lecturer and linguist.

This biographical study focuses on Nketia's educational background, his work as a scholar and his career as a teacher and music educator. It does not deal with his career as a composer (for which his countrymen, Ghanaians, know him best) for, at the time work on this study was in progress, I was aware that the distinguished Nigerian musicologist, composer and pianist, Professor Akin Euba, who succeeded Professor Nketia as Andrew W. Mellon Professor of Music at the University of Pittsburgh, U.S.A. in 1991, was writing a book under the title, Bridging Ethnomusicology and Composition: A Study of J.H. Nketia, devoted to this aspect of Nketia's life.

This biographical study is presented in two parts: part one deals with his educational background and his work as a teacher and scholar at the Presbyterian Training College, Akropong, the University of Ghana, Legon, the University of California at Los Angeles, U.S.A., the University of Pittsburgh, U.S.A., and finally at the International Centre for African Music and Dance, also at the University of Ghana, Legon: and part two is devoted to the educational value of his source materials, such as his books on African Musicology, his thoughts on music education found in his articles, and the practical application of ethnomusicology and composition in his pedagogical pieces and exercises in African rhythm.

November 2001

Eric A. Akrofi
Umtata, South Africa

CHAPTER ONE

MUSICAL EDUCATION AND THE FORMATIVE PERIOD OF HIS LIFE (1928-1952)

Joseph Hanson Kwabena Nketia was born on June 22, 1921 at Mampong in the Ashanti Region of Ghana. He was the only child of his father, Akwasi Yeboa and his mother, Akua Adoma who were traders at Effiduase, a cocoa centre town near Mampong. He, therefore, spent his early childhood years with his parents at Effiduase where he saw and enjoyed performances of traditional Ghanaian music. He was particularly fascinated by the music of popular performing groups known as "Sika-rebewu-ɛpere"[1] and saw several performances by such ensembles at Effiduase and Asokore, a nearby town.

Since his father died in his infancy, Kwabena Nketia was reared by his mother and maternal grandparents. When he was seven years old, his mother decided that he should go and stay with his grand-parents at Mampong and start school. His grandparents were Christians who belonged to the Presbyterian Church. His grandfather, Opanyin Kisi Amoa, who, as a Senior Presbyter, held an influential position in the church, and his grandmother, Yaa Amankwaa, lived in an area called "Sukuu mu"[2] the location of the Basel Mission. They took care of him but Kwabena Nketia discovered, when he grew up, that his mother regularly sent them money for his primary school education. After his primary school education, his mother appealed to her brother, Yaw Gyimah, Kwabena's uncle, to look after him while he was in middle and senior school.

As Christians, Kwabena Nketia's grandparents and uncle who reared him were not permitted to participate in performances of traditional music which the church regarded as primitive and pagan. However, the continued adherence of his mother and other relatives to traditional customs and ways of life provided for him a broad range of musical practices and styles in Akan life (DjeDje and Carter, 1989:3).

Kwabena Nketia commuted by lorry between Mampong and Effiduase to visit his grandmother. He recalls that although his mother was not a member of any of the traditional performing groups he had seen in his early childhood, she joined performances given by groups such as adowa[3] and nnwonkoro[4] when she attended funerals and other social functions. The active participation in traditional musical performances by other members of his lineage also helped him in later years to know and understand Akan[5] music as well as traditional songs.

Kwabena Nketia is grateful to his mother and other relatives for providing him with an exposure to Akan traditional music in his childhood. According to him, he was lucky to have had a parent and relatives who, as Christians, had no conflict of interest in attending church and performances of traditional music concurrently, and therefore, encouraged him to perform as well as study such music. (Interview with author in July 1999).

1. *Primary and Middle School Music Education (1928-1936)*

"Throughout primary and middle school years in Mampong, Nketia showed exceptional talent and sensitivity to music, dance, poetry and dramatic arts". (DjeDje and Carter, 1989:3). His formal music education began at the Mampong Asante Presbyterian Junior School where he learnt to sing Western songs and church hymns and also to write tonic sol-fa notation. He copied songs written in tonic sol-fa notation on the blackboard by his teacher and learnt them at home.

In Senior School he sang treble in the choir and was responsible for giving the pitch for songs during singing practices. He, therefore, played a very significant role in the school's musical activities. He acquired a repertoire of western songs and Christian hymns which were taught in Presbyterian schools in those days. He also had his first experience with the music of the renowned Ghanaian composer, Ephraim Amu, whose choral piece; "Yaanom Abibirimma" had a great effect on him.

Kwabena Nketia's great interest in music urged him to seek more musical knowledge outside his school premises. He received tuition from Mr H.T. Dako, a native of Begoro who had studied music at the

Presbyterian Training College, Akropong founded in 1848 by the Basel Mission. Dako who was then on the staff of the Middle School at Mampong, taught him some Western songs that were in vogue in the 1930s and accompanied him on the bandoneon.

Mr. Charles William Gyima, a school teacher and nephew of Kwabena Nketia's grandparents who lived in the same family house, owned a harmonium which he played early in the morning. Kwabena enjoyed the music played on it but was not allowed to touch the instrument. He later developed an interest in the harmonium and was determined to learn to play it as a result of a musical performance he attended. Three Mampong students, who were studying music at the Presbyterian Training College at Akropong, gave an evening concert when they came home for holidays. Their repertoire comprised mainly of songs by Ephraim Amu who was the music teacher at the college at that time. Kwabena Nketia was deeply moved by the performance of "Bonwere Kentenwene" Amu's famous song for solo voice and piano (performed on the harmonium at the concert).

Kwabena Nketia was such an intelligent pupil at school that he completed the ten-year elementary school course in nine years. In his last year at school in 1936, his headteacher, Mr Edward Addo Danso, advised and convinced him to take the national entrance examination for the Presbyterian Training College, Akropong. He passed with distinction placing second among a group of several hundred students who took the examination. This earned him admission to the college in 1937. His uncle, Yaw Gyima, was not happy about this development because he wanted him, upon completion of his elementary education, to work as a store assistant or find a job in a store in Kumasi, Ghana's second largest city and the commercial centre of the Ashanti Region of Ghana.

2. *The Formative Period of his Career (1937-1952)*

"As for the formative period of my life, I place considerable weight on Akropong Presbyterian Training College" (Letter dated May 5, 1999 from Nketia to the author).

2.1 The Akropong Years (1937-1944)

After his education at the local primary and middle schools at Mampong, Kwabena Nketia left his hometown for the Presbyterian Training College at Akropong-Akwapim in the Eastern Region of Ghana to be trained as a teacher. He studied several subjects but was especially interested in Music and Twi (a dialect of Akan). He studied music under his mentor Robert Danso, a well-known theory teacher and organist, whose style of playing the harmonium inspired him.

Under the tutorship of Robert Danso, Kwabena Nketia's playing of the harmonium improved so much that during his second year at Akropong he played the instrument at church services both at the College and the Presbyterian Church in town. According to Nketia, (interview with author in July 1999) during his second and third years at the College he became an unofficial assistant to Robert Danso who asked him to copy music on the blackboard for his (Danso's) music lessons. Also, anytime Robert Danso could not go to church in town he asked him to play the harmonium for the service. As a substitute organist for Robert Danso, Kwabena Nketia's performance on the harmonium was so good and similar in style to that of the former that only very few among the congregation would notice that it was he (Nketia) and not their church organist (Danso) who was at the keyboard on such occasions.

Kwabena Nketia did not only learn to play the harmonium at Akropong but also studied the Theory of Music (limited to the rudiments of Western music), which was a compulsory subject for students at the College. To improve his keyboard skill and knowledge of theory, he copied pieces from Smallwoods Pianoforte Tutor[6] in a drawing book and practised them on the harmonium during his school holidays at Mampong.

Another musical theorist, who was also a composer, who contributed to the musical development of Kwabena Nketia during these years, was Otto Boateng, a resident of Larteh, a town eight kilometres away from Akropong. Nketia recalls that it was Otto Boateng who gave him a copy of a book on harmony written by Stewart Macpherson, to study on his own. He found the book so useful that he ordered a copy of another book by the same author, entitled Melody and Harmony, studied it, and tried to do the exercises prescribed in it.

In his third year at Akropong, Kwabena Nketia was sent by Robert Danso to teach choirs in parts of the town. This encouraged him to write his own music for such groups known as singing bands. Most of what he wrote then consisted of hymns and marching songs in a Western idiom with Twi texts. These he considered as preparatory compositions and started to write more serious pieces after he left college (Akrofi, 1992:41).

Kwabena Nketia emphasizes that it was not only his teachers who made contributions to his musical development. One of his classmates at Akropong, Nomo Jones, a native of the coastal town of Ada in the Greater Accra Region of Ghana, influenced him. Nomo was a very good pianist of jazz and popular music and was fond of ragtime. Nketia's pianism-style which he developed in the 1960s through the 1970s, is the result of the influence from Nomo James (Interview with author, July 1999).

An incident in Kwabena Nketia's third year at the Presbyterian Training College set him off into researching into traditional Ghanaian songs. As he recalls (Vieta, 1999:446):

> In my third year at Akropong, our English teacher, Mr Beveridge was telling us about English prosody and used terms such as iambic, trochaic and dactylic pentameter which fascinated me. Later, I asked myself whether we had similar things in Akan prosody. As I could not find the answer, I tried to write down some of the traditional songs I had learnt as a child at

Mampong with the purpose of analysing them to find iambic and trochaic pentameters, but was disappointed. This led me to develop great interest in collecting more traditional songs in order to acquaint myself with the distinctive features of poetry and prose styles in traditional society.

In 1941 Kwabena Nketia completed the Training College and graduated as a Certificated Trained Teacher (Cert.A). He was appointed a member of staff at the College in 1942 to teach Music and Twi. In addition to his teaching duties, he worked as an assistant to C.A. Akrofi, the Chief Editor for Twi, appointed by the Government Department of Education to examine, edit and write reports on all manuscripts submitted to it before they were published. The literary and scholarly interest he developed early in his career was stimulated to a large extent by this work. In Nketia's words (Vieta, 1999:446) :

> Experience gained in this work enabled me to prepare the texts of the songs I had collected into a publishable manuscript. This anthology of over a hundred Akan songs completed in 1944 was later published in 1949 by Oxford University Press. That was my first book in musicology.

In 1942, while still serving as a tutor at the College, Nketia met for the first time Ephraim Amu,

w

whose compositions he had heard in his childhood and teenage years. Amu, who had returned from Britain where he studied composition at the Royal College of Music in London, had come on a visit to the Presbyterian Training College where he taught Music in the 1920's and 1930s before Nketia was admitted as a student there. He attended the College morning service for which Nketia played the harmonium. After the service, Amu, who had heard about Nketia's achievement in musical composition, jokingly said to him, "Young man, I gather you are interested in composition. Don't copy my music!"

After his first meeting with Amu, Nketia was encouraged by Rev. G.K. Ampofo, a member of staff at the Presbyterian Training College, who was a nephew of Amu, to visit Amu at Achimota, near Accra. On one of his visits to Amu, Kwabena Nketia observed the composer at work for two weeks. Amu encouraged him to play J.S. Bach's Two Part Inventions on the piano at his home and insisted that he practised while he (Amu) was teaching in the classroom. He also showed Nketia his notebooks which contained field notes, poems, Akan phrases and texts, and tonic sol-fa notation of the tunes he used in his musical compositions, especially songs and choral pieces. Nketia was fascinated by some of the material he found in Amu's notebooks, especially, Akan phraseology and poetic images culled from traditional Akan songs. He still remembers some of them which he uses for illustration in his lectures.

During the two-week period when he was a guest at Amu's home, Nketia also learnt that his host got inspiration for his compositions from his regular walks in a park on the campus of Achimota College where he taught music. Nketia tried to see if walking in the park would inspire him too, but he was distracted by the squirrels and singing of the birds. According to Nketia (Vieta, 1999:446) his visits to Amu's home :

> ...began a long period of friendship. On each occasion that I visited Amu, he inspired me to do further research and compose new songs. But he almost always advised me not to copy his style but develop my own. Amu became my model from that time.

In 1944, after almost three years of teaching at the Presbyterian Training College, Kwabena Nketia was awarded a two-year scholarship to study linguistics at the University of London in the Africa Department of the School of Oriental and African Studies. Amu expressed concern that he was not awarded a scholarship for music when Nketia broke the news to him. He confessed to Nketia later that he had a sleepless night on the day that he heard the news, worrying that Nketia might lose his musical talent if he studied any subject other than music. He had shared his musical knowledge and experience with Nketia and was afraid that the wonderful academic relationship they had developed would not last if his younger friend did not choose music for a career.

According to DjeDje and Carter (1989:6), the manuscript of Akan songs Nketia produced in 1944 earned him the scholarship to study in London:

This manuscript (completed in 1944 and published five years later by Oxford University Press) came to the notice of Professor Ida Ward, Head of the Africa Department of the School of Oriental and African Studies of the University of London when she came to Ghana at the invitation of the colonial government to investigate into some dialectal problems in Akan and suggest appropriate changes in the orthography in Twi. On her recommendation, Nketia was awarded a two-year scholarship to study modern linguistics at the University of London in the Africa Department of the School of Oriental and African Studies.

2.2 *The London Years (1944-1949)*

Between 1944 and 1946 Kwabena Nketia studied Linguistics and Social Anthropology at the School of Oriental and African Studies (SOAS) at the University of London. Since he was still interested in Music, he decided, to continue studying Western music which he believed, would enhance his knowledge of traditional African music. As Nketia (see Vieta, 1999:447) says:

> I wanted to learn as much Western music as possible so that I would be able to enjoy the best of two worlds. I, however, refused to be overwhelmed by Western music, for my first obligation and loyalty was to the music of my own people.

He took private piano lessons, continued with studies in harmony and counterpoint which he had begun in Ghana, attended orchestral concerts at the Royal Albert Hall as well as piano recitals and music concerts at Wigmore Hall. He also joined a choral society and an international students' organisation which enabled him to have access to cheaper concert tickets and also socialise with some artists, composers and promoters in London.

After successfully completing his course in Phonetics and Linguistics in 1946, Kwabena Nketia was employed for a period of three years, as an assistant in the Department of Africa at SOAS to help in the language training of young British cadets destined to become officers in the British colonies of West Africa. In spite of his new demanding job he found time to study music at Trinity College of Music (London) and also registered for a three-year degree programme in Music, English and History at Birkbeck College. Nketia had many irons in the fire. It was during this time that he acquired his life-long habit of working several hours a day on different tasks.

Kwabena Nketia met his mentor, Professor John R. Firth, during his tenure at the Department of Africa. When Professor Firth, the first Professor of Linguistics to be appointed Chair of General Linguistics at the School of Oriental and African Studies, University of London, learned from his colleagues about the good work of Nketia, he advised the latter to take his course in the Phonetics of English. He also encouraged Nketia to do intensive work in Linguistic analysis at both undergraduate and postgraduate levels. In fact, Nketia is thankful to Firth (as we will find in chapter six, p.121 of this study) for making him aware of the "heuristic value of context and contextual analysis".

2.3   Return to Ghana/Akropong

In 1949 Kwabena Nketia obtained a B.A. degree from the University of London and thereafter returned to Ghana and rejoined the staff of the Presbyterian Training College, Akropong to teach Music and English. He also worked at the Language Bureau (now Bureau of Ghana Languages) with C.A. Akrofi (with whom he had earlier worked between 1942 and 1944) on research projects in Twi orthography. He made an immense contribution to the development of Twi language education during his three-year tenure (1949-1952) at the Bureau. His revision of the *Twi Spelling Book* (which contains all the lexical entries in Christaller's standard *Twi Dictionary* first published in 1881) and all the six Primary School Readers used in those days are excellent examples of his work. As a member of the Presbyterian Literature Committee, Kwabena Nketia had to edit manuscripts and translate a few English educational pamplets such as "The Story of Healing" and "The Story of Flying" for publication in Twi. This resulted in the publication of *Mframa mu Akwantuo Ho Mpanisɛm* (translation of "The Story of Flying") by the Presbyterian Book Depot, Accra 1951 and 1952 respectively. The experience he gained from his research on Twi orthography was instrumental in his collection of Akan songs in the field which resulted in the publication of his *Akanfoɔ Nnwom Bi* by Oxford University Press in 1949. Kwabena Nketia also wrote supplementary readers in Twi for schools. These were mainly original stories or anthologies of short stories from traditional history. Again, in 1949, Oxford University published his *Akanfoɔ Anansesɛm*, an edition of folk tales about the ubiquitous Ananse. His very productive work in Twi literature earned him another influential position when he was appointed a member of the Advisory Board of the Vernacular Literature Bureau in 1950. He continued to work assiduously and wrote *Ananwona* (an Akan play) and *Kwabena Amoa* (fiction) both of which were published by Oxford University Press. By producing ten publications (one on music and the rest on Twi literature) in a short period of two and a half years (1949-1952), Kwabena Nketia showed in the formative years of his career that he was not only a prolific writer and an expert on Akan language but was also versed in Akan customs and culture. It was not only Akans, but all Ghanaians also benefited immensely from Nketia's output during the formative period of his life. Djedje and Carter (1989:8) aptly described this period of his career as follows:

> In addition Kwabena Nketia is also widely known in Ghana as a composer, for the period 1942-1952 when he wrote books in his own

language was also the period in which he wrote many of his choral pieces and solos with piano accompaniment which are broadcast quite frequently by the Ghana Broadcasting and Television Corporation.

In fact, Nketia's best known composition, *Yaanom Montie* was one of the songs he wrote before he studied and worked in London. It was recorded by national radio and has been used as a musical interlude or signature tune for some radio music programmes since the 1950s.

Kwabena Nketia became Acting Principal of the Presbyterian Training College, Akropong, his alma mater, in 1952, a position he held only for a brief period because he had to leave the same year for a research fellowship position at the University College of the Gold Coast, established in 1948 and first sited on the campus of Achimota where he had visited Ephraim Amu in the early 1940s.

CHAPTER TWO

NKETIA AND HIS FAMILY (1951-)

On January 6, 1951, Kwabena Nketia married Lily Agyeman-Dua at Mampong. He had known her since his childhood. In fact, they were next door neighbours at Mampong.

Wedding picture taken on 6th January, 1951
Mr. and Mrs. Nketia

*Group picture taken at the wedding on 6th January, 1951
Mr. and Mrs Nketia in the middle, front row*

*Nketia family, 1957
left to right-front row: Naana, Akosua, the late Kwabena (KB)
Back row: Lily Nketia*

Lily started her career as a teacher and later worked as a producer and rose to the rank of Assistant Controller of Programmes before her retirement from the Ghana Broadcasting Corporation in Accra, Ghana's capital. She was a distinguished radio host for the programmes "Women's World" and "A Time with Children".

Four children were born from this marriage. The eldest child, Dr. Akosua Perbi (née Nketia) was born in 1952, and is currently a Senior Lecturer in History and head of department at the University of Ghana. Kwabena (deceased) and Naana, the second and third children, are both lawyers while Kwame, the youngest, is a businessman resident in the United States of America.

Akosua and Kwabena are the more musical of the children. Akosua studied music in secondary school and was a very good dancer of traditional Ghanaian music performed at school. Kwabena enjoyed playing the guitar and as a school boy, played the instrument in one of the popular music groups in vogue in Ghanaian secondary schools during the 1960s Kwabena Nketia did not discourage any of his children from studying music. However, he was indifferent to any of them taking up music as a profession. Of his four children, only Akosua really became interested in music and studied it seriously. According to Akosua (letter dated 25th November, 1999 to the author) :

> So far as my interest in Music is concerned, I think first it was running through my blood, second, I saw my father play the piano as well

as have rehearsals with Prof. Laing and Mr Simmons in our home. A few concerts were also held in our home. When I was in primary school, an African-American lady who came to work for some time at the Institute of African Studies, came home to teach me how to play the piano. It was Daddy who asked her to teach me, because he did not have time to give me lessons. When I played the piano and he was at home he did correct me whenever I made mistakes. It was this interest which carried me through Achimota School.

Mr D.R. Essah, Akosua's music teacher at Achimota School played a role in her musical education. Akosua recalls (letter of 25th November 1999):

> As soon as he met me and realised that I was the daughter of Prof. Nketia, he was so excited about it. He told me Daddy taught him music at the Presbyterian Training College, Akropong. He encouraged me to do the A.B.R.S.M. theory of music as well as the piano exams. I think in both cases I got up to Grade 3. Then he insisted I do 'O' level music. My protests fell on deaf ears and I did not do well in this examination.

Akosua also remembers that because of her father's fame as a musician and a composer she was expected to take an active role in musical activities when she studied at Achimota School in the 1960s. In her first year at the school she had to conduct her House choir (Kingsley House Choir) for an inter-house singing competition in the 1964/65 academic year. "Then again because of my name, I was forced to take part in Cultural Dancing from Form 1 to 5. Every Founder's Day, I was there, in front of the Administration Block dancing. I also joined the School Choir from Form 1-5". (ibid)

Akosua's interest in music continued after she left school. She still sings and enjoys music but says "it has been a long while since I played the piano". (ibid). She has encouraged all her four children (grandchildren of Kwabena Nketia) to take private lessons in piano, theory of music, atenteben and voice. When her third child, a little girl, expressed interest in playing the traditional xylophone (gyil) after she had seen one in her grandfather's office, her grandfather ordered a metallic one to be made for her.

Akosua has childhood memories of her father's predilection for work as can be seen from the following statement:

> Daddy has been a workaholic ever since I saw him. He was always the first to get up in the morning and the last to go to bed. I remember him locking doors and turning off lights when I was cosy in bed. I remember him in his study in the quiet of the night writing or humming some

notes he is putting down while I was in bed. (ibid.)

On Kwabena Nketia's daily routine Akosua writes :

> He usually left the house at 8:00 am for work, came home for lunch around 12:30 –1:00 pm, rested awhile in the sitting room chair and went back to work around 2:00 pm. At 4:00 pm he would come back for tea, relax a bit and go back to work. Sometimes he would come back at about 7:00 pm. After supper, he would relax a bit in the sitting room and go back to the study. If he watched television and listened to the radio it was only for news. That has been his lifestyle and it appears it still is. He is now 78 but the old man has not changed. He still leaves home about 8 – 8:30 am, goes home for lunch, rests a while and goes back to work. In between teaching he has numerous meetings he attends.

The statement above attests to Kwabena Nketia's habit of working several hours a day which he acquired during the years he studied in London. Akosua recalls that the Nketia family had an elderly woman house helper some years ago. After staying with them for some time she (the helper) made the following remark in Twi about her father, *"Nti Papa de nwoma no nkoaa!"* (translation – "How come Papa spends all his time reading books").

When Kwabena Nketia retired from the University of Ghana in 1979 and was moving his family from his university accommodation to his own house at Madina, near the university campus, there was a little quarrel between him and his dear wife over the furniture for their new home. Lily complained to their daughter, Akosua, that after they had bought new beds and were thinking of the furniture for the sitting room, her father wanted a writing desk and a chair for his study purchased first, before the sitting room furniture. She asked Akosua whether this was good logic. While Lily was worried about where the visitors they received immediately after they settled in their new home would sit, Kwabena Nketia's preoccupation was the furniture for his academic work.

Lily has, for almost half a century of their marriage, been a wonderful wife to Kwabena Nketia and a very caring mother to their four children. Akosua, the eldest child writes :

> Mama has been the pillar at home when the old man spends the better part of his time on his books or travelled all over the world. He is still travelling. As I write, he has left for Nigeria. (letter of 25th November, 1999 to the author).

Kwabena Nketia attributes his success in life partly to his family when he says:

> It lies in diligence and devotion, that is, making your career (or whatever you pursue as well as what you cherish in life, including your family) an integral part of your way of life and a stimulus for reflection and creativity. (Vieta, 1999:450)

Picture of Nketia nuclear family taken on the 70th birthday of Lily, September 16th, 1998
Left to right: Kwame, Akosua, the late Kwabena, Nketia, Naana, Lily

CHAPTER THREE

THE LEGON YEARS (1952 - 1979)

In 1952, Kwabena Nketia was appointed a Research Fellow in African Studies in the Department of Sociology, University College of the Gold Coast (University College of Ghana, 1957 - 1961). He was invited by Professor Kofi Abrefa Busia, Head of the Department of Sociology, (who became Ghana's Prime Minister, 1969 - 1972) who was interested in developing cultural studies at the University, especially in African traditions, music and related arts at the degree level.

According to Nketia (1970a:9) his appointment gave birth to ethnomusicology in Ghana:

> It was fortunate for us in Ghana that when the University College of Ghana was established, there was a Ghanaian Head of the Department of Sociology who was interested in developing cultural studies on the campus. Although the Principal of the University College admitted that he did not quite understand the programme that was envisaged, he had enough respect for the wisdom of that Head of Department to allow him to go ahead. In 1952, ethnomusicology finally came to the University as it were, by the back door through the Department of Sociology.

His appointment also offered him the opportunity to continue his research in linguistics, music and dance. But he decided to focus on the research into traditional African music he had begun in the 1940s, "for he believed that music would give him the greatest scope for studying the expressive cultures of his people and for realizing his interdisciplinary background and interest" (DjeDje and Carter, 1989:8). He, therefore, did intensive field research on the music and literature of the Akan people of Ghana. One of the first things he did in his new job was to start a small library at the Sociology Department with his field collections. He later supplemented these with commercial recordings of music including early highlife[8] records which he thought would be useful historical material some day (see Nketia, 1970:9).

Nketia's hard work resulted in the publication of his second book in musicology, *Funeral Dirges of the Akan People,* which was published in 1955. According to DjeDje and Carter (1989:9) Nketia's methodology for building interdisciplinary bridges and establishing a relationship between linguistic analysis and translation, evident in this book, caught the attention of his mentor, Professor J.R. Firth, who praised his work.

Between 1952 and 1961, Kwabena Nketia published profusely when he produced over forty papers in local and international newspapers and journals. Ten of the papers, on drums and language, musical instruments, and African music and culture appeared in the most popular daily newspaper in Ghana, The Daily Graphic, in 1961. Earlier, in 1956, two of his papers: "The Gramophone and Contemporary African Music in the Gold Coast" and "The Role of the Drummer in Akan Society" were published in Ibadan, Nigeria where he had read them at conferences. Another of his papers, titled "Yoruba Musicians in Accra" was also published in Ibadan in 1958. Some of his scholarly writings read at conferences, beyond the shores of Africa, notably "Possession Dances in African Societies" and "Changing Traditions of Folk Music in Ghana" were published in 1957 and 1959 respectively in the *Journal of the International Folk Music Council.*

Kwabena Nketia's activities in the 1950s were not confined to field research and the writing of books and papers. He played an important role in national affairs relating to the development of arts and culture. According to DjeDje and Carter (1989:9) "Because this was a period of general awakening in Ghana as well as a period of transition from colonial rule to independence, he took an active part in the cultural movements of that period and the work of the Arts Council of Ghana aimed at reinstating the traditional arts in contemporary life." Indeed, Nketia was a member of the Interim Committee for the Arts Council of Ghana in 1955, member of the Arts Council of Ghana in 1961, and subsequently became Chairman of the Council from 1976 -1979. His association with the Arts Council since the 1950s earned him an invitation from government to take part in the planning of cultural activities for the Republic celebration of his country on July 1, 1960 after gaining independence from Britain on March 6, 1957. This encouraged him to invite traditional Ghanaian drum and horn ensembles to perform music in addition to the Western military fanfares provided by military or police bequeathed to the country by the British colonial government.

Kwabena Nketia (1991:88) sums up what he was able to achieve in his early years at the University of Ghana as follows:

> Working in an academic environment but believing very strongly in the need for making my research relevant to my own community, I was able to formulate research paradigms that enabled me to pursue my scholarly interests in areas in which I could make some contribution to knowledge and understanding of African music while making certain types of information and materials accessible to my own people. I involved myself in the reconstruction of our state ceremonies because of my knowledge of Ghanaian traditions. In addition I contributed articles on music and culture to local newspapers and the radio, prepared and published annotated texts of funeral dirges, praise poetry of the Akan court, drum language, the repertoire of Akan hunters songs and other materials for use as textbooks in Akan language and literature courses.

In 1958, Kwabena Nketia founded the Ghana Music Society with a group of Ghanaian music academics, researchers and musicians. According to him (Nketia, 1970:22), the Society was formed "in order that we can share our experiences with all music lovers and stimulate general interest in the development of music in Ghana".

Also in the same year, 1958, he was offered a Rockefeller Foundation Fellowship to study composition and musicology in the United States of America. He studied in New York, at the Juilliard School of Music and also at Columbia University with the composer, Henry Cowell. He also took a course in organology taught by Curt Sachs whose works he had read.

While in the United States, Kwabena Nketia also came into contact with Melville Herskovits whom he had met in Ghana and Alan Merriam whom he first met at a conference in Belgium. Both of them taught him ethnomusicology for one semester at Northwestern University where he also audited courses in the Anthropology Department. In addition to his studies in composition, ethnomusicology and anthropology Nketia had the opportunity to visit several institutions of music as well as meet some famous American ethnomusicologists and composers. Some of the institutions he visited were the Archive of Traditional Music at Indiana University, Bloomington, Princeton University and the Institute of Ethnomusicology at the University of California at Los Angeles (UCLA).

Among the distinguished scholars and composers he met were Milton Babbit, Mieczyslaw Kolinski, George Herzog, Roger Sessions and Mantle Hood. He discovered during his study tour of America that most of the scholars he met shared a common ideal which was "a strong commitment to studies that integrate music, society and culture from different conceptual and analytical perspectives, a commitment that enabled them in spite of their differences, to share in the knowledge and insight gained by individual scholars working on different musical materials and cultures at home and abroad." (DjeDje and Carter 1989:9). Nketia realised that he had a similar commitment in connection with his work in Ghana. His collaboration with musicians, dancers, choreographers, and other artists during his early years at the University of Ghana, urged him to adopt an interdisciplinary approach to his research methodology.

When he returned from his one-year study tour of the United States, Kwabena Nketia was compelled to move his programme from the Sociology Department of the University of Ghana. Although his work in that department progressed steadily, in 1959, "the new Head of Department, a non-Ghanaian who found it somewhat embarrassing to have to look after ethnomusicology in his department, conveniently arranged for it to be housed in the Department of Archeology, ostensibly for lack of space in the Sociology Department" (Nketia 1970:10). This development, which was the first move to separate cultural studies from sociology in Ghana, did not discourage Nketia from working relentlessly to keep ethnomusicology alive in the University. Neither did he have to wait too long for a permanent department for his programme. In 1961, the University of Ghana established an Institute of African Studies, and there his programme finally found its home. It was no longer tied to the shoestrings of a non-fine arts department (Akrofi, 1992:43). Kwabena Nketia, who had been promoted a Senior Research Fellow in 1959, assumed responsibility for the Music and Related Arts section of the Institute, and in this semi-autonomous position, he was able to strengthen and subsequently expand the ethnomusicology programme in the University. He arranged for the library of collections he established in the Sociology Department in the 1950s to be transferred to the Institute where it was expanded, with a grant from the Rockefeller Foundation, to hold tape recordings of traditional music from all parts of Ghana and other countries in Africa.

As head of the Music and Related Arts section of the Institute, Kwabena Nketia collaborated and shared ideas with Research Fellows of the other sections of the Institute, namely African Languages, History, Social Studies, and Government and Politics in Africa. He arranged for music to be included as one of the electives in the interdisciplinary postgraduate degree courses of the Institute and also instituted a special two-year diploma in African music course for people who already had diplomas (or their equivalent) in Western music. Among the first graduates of the latter course were Ben Aning, Michael Amissah, N.Z. Nayo,

S.D. Asiama and Nissio Fiagbedzi, who later became distinguished Ghanaian ethnomusicologists or composers. In 1962, a School of Music, Dance and Drama was established as part of the Institute of African Studies with Kwabena Nketia, (who had been promoted to the rank of Associate Professor in the same year) as its director. Nketia (1970:10) recalls that the School was established "in order to provide an outlet for the use of research materials accumulated over the years and to stimulate new areas of research, creative work and teaching in African music and related arts". Facilities for undergraduate studies in music were also provided in the School. A three-year general diploma in music course for post-secondary school students proficient in music was instituted. It involved the study of both African and Western music. Some of the graduates of this course were encouraged or helped by Kwabena Nketia to pursue post-graduate studies especially in the United States. Among them are distinguished Ghanaian academics like W.K. Amoaku, N.N. Kofie and Daniel Avorgbedor who are all musicologists.

    The Institute of African Studies received a subsidy from the Ministry of Culture which required it to promote the performing arts of Ghana, and especially to establish a National Dance Company. To achieve this objective, Kwabena Nketia and the Ghanaian choreographer, Albert Mawere Opoku, his close friend and collaborator, recruited traditional dance teachers, dancers, drummers and musicians from the major ethnic groups in Ghana. They made these artists full-time employees of the Institute and this enabled the drummers to play for the dancers every working day.

This group of performers changed the cultural orientation of the University of Ghana, for the music of academic processions during congregation (graduation) which was provided by the Police Band in the pre-independence period, was now performed by not only drummers and dancers of traditional African music but also the local bamboo flute (atenteben) ensemble of the Institute. Kwabena Nketia, therefore, succeeded in bringing live, stimulating traditional African music to a university campus which had not experienced such a thing before. He was not discouraged by the nickname 'dondology'[9], "that students and others overwhelmed by the sudden appearance of African drums on the hallowed precincts of the University of Ghana derisively gave to the studies in music and drama and by implication, to the discipline of ethnomusicology most directly concerned with these studies. For them, it was not only a strange field but a big joke, for they could not by any stretch of imagination believe there is more to ethnomusicology than the aural manifestation of it". (Nketia, 1970:23).

In fact it took over a decade for university lecturers and students to accept the study of African music, especially drumming and dancing, as serious academic work.

Kwabena Nketia's outstanding work at both the Institute of African Studies and the School of Music, Dance and Drama earned him international recognition which resulted in invitations to academic institutions interested in the field of ethnomusicology, especially the music of Africa. In 1963, the African Studies Program at the University of California at Los Angeles (UCLA) invited him to teach a summer course on the music of Africa. This invitation enabled him to establish regular contact with the institution and this resulted in his appointment as Professor of Music in 1968 after which he became a regular member of the Department of Music and the Institute of Ethnomusicology at UCLA. Also in 1963, the University of Ghana promoted him to the rank of full professor for his meritorious service to the university as well as his numerous publications.

In 1965, Kwabena Nketia was appointed Director of the Institute of African Studies (a position he held for fifteen years, until his retirement in 1979). He combined his new position with the directorship of both the School of Music, Dance and Drama and the Dance Company. One of his remarkable achievements in these years was the development of the Dance Company he and Mawere Opoku started in 1962 into the Ghana Dance Ensemble which was inaugurated in 1967. He strongly felt that dance and music were inseparable in the African context as can be seen in the following statement :

> African music and dance are inseparable and no African ethnomusicological programme can afford to neglect the visual dimension of this music which influences its conception as well as its interpretation and function. (Nketia, 1970:19)

He expected the Ghana Dance Ensemble to play an important part in the training programmes of the Institute of African Studies, workshops organised occasionally for researchers and educators; and the Institute's extension programme in the arts for the community. Professor Mawere Opoku, the eminent Ghanaian dance teacher and choreographer who assisted him in the formation of the Ensemble has this to say about Kwabena Nketia :

> I started working with him at the Institute as far back as 1963. He was then director of the Ghana Dance Ensemble of which I was the artistic director. I must say in his capacity as director he provided me and my aides with all the necessary facilities that enabled me to collect materials which helped me to choreograph some of the dances currently in use in the country. That facility was not given to me alone but to other research colleagues in the Institute. Nketia as the director of the Institute used his contacts and his standing as an academic of repute to secure funding for projects. Land Rovers and recording equipment and funds were at the disposal of all staff for collecting materials from all over the country. These materials later found their way into our lecture notes or became publications which were deposited in the Institute's archives. The extensive collection of materials from all over the country and even outside gave the Institute

an international respect which was reflected in the way researchers from all over the world flock to the Institute year in year out. (Vieta, 1999:448)

Apart from Mawere Opoku, Kwabena Nketia invited other Ghanaian researchers or composers of African music like Ephraim Amu (whom he had known in his youth), Atta Annan Mensah, Ben Aning, N.Z. Nayo and Nissio Fiagbedzi to name only a few, to work with him at either the Institute of African Studies or the School of Music, Dance and Drama. Although some of these persons were his former students (for example Fiagbedzi whom he taught between 1964 and 1966) he treated them as equals and shared knowledge and experiences with them. Fiagbedzi (1989:45) writes:

> When in 1970 I joined the academic staff of the Music Department, Professor Nketia had already been the Director of the Institute of African Studies and the School of Music, Dance and Drama for at least five years. As Director he drew around him students and cultural scientists from all over the world, and he was Visiting Professor at UCLA where he went every year to lecture... Many were the times that Professor and I exchanged views on various issues in African music research at Legon, during his African music seminars at UCLA and informally at other times. One such occasion was in 1974 when Professor invited me (I was then a doctoral

student at UCLA) to help him with some material he was working on for his latest book, *The Music of Africa*. It was an encouragement to discover later that the little I was able to do for his purpose was enough to make him cite my name in the Preface.

Kwabena Nketia appointed the composers and researchers he invited to work with him as Research Fellows and collaborated with them. One product of such collaboration was the journal named *Papers in African Studies*. The third volume of this journal, published in 1968 by the Institute of African Studies, contains articles on African music based on research conducted by Nketia himself, Atta Annan Mensah, N.Z Nayo and Ben Aning. Also, because of his interdisciplinary background, Kwabena Nketia was able to work closely with other Research Fellows at the Institute who were not necessarily experts in the fields of music, dance and drama. Thus he was able to publish many papers on a plethora of topics in related disciplines, based on material he obtained from his fieldwork and other sources connected with music. Such publications, produced between 1962 and 1974, include articles on "Worship in West African Religions", "Prayers at Kple Worship", "The Artist in Contemporary Africa : The Challenge of Tradition", "Historical Evidence in Ga Religious Music", "National Theatre Movements and the African Image", "The Techniques of African Oral Literature", "The Creative Arts and the Community", "Changing Patterns of Performer-Audience Relationship",

"The Linguistic Aspect of Style in African Languages", "Universities as Centres of the Creative Arts" and "Surrogate Languages of Africa".

The fruits of Nketia's arduous work at the Institute of African Studies during the 1960s also manifested themselves in publications such as *African Music in Ghana* (1962), *Drumming in Akan Communities of Ghana* (1963), *Folk Songs of Ghana* (1963). These, like his two earlier publications; *Akanfoɔ Nnwom Bi* (1949) *and Funeral Dirges of the Akan People* (1955) are books in musicology. His other publications such as : *Ghana: Music, Dance and Drama* (1965) *and Our Drums and Drummers* (1968) are booklets "intended to broaden the layman's knowledge about the performing arts in Ghana". (Akrofi, 1992:44).

Also, in the 1960s, Kwabena Nketia wrote his own music to serve the needs of the School of Music, Dance and Drama. He wrote short pieces for the atenteben ensemble as well as a few Western instruments. Pieces such as *Owora* (1965), *At the Cross Roads* (1961), *Dagarti Work Song* (1967) and *Volta Fantasy* (1967), all piano solos; two quartets for *atenteben, Three Ghanaian Airs for violin and piano; Three Arrangements of Highlife Tunes and Antubam* for cello and piano were written for staff and student instrumentalists at the school, which Nketia (1970:19) described as "an experiment in training in bimusicality", and to achieve this objective, he and other composers like Amu, Mensah and Nayo tried to encourage Ghanaian and foreign staff of the school to perform both African and Western music or their compositions which combined elements of both cultures.

Kwabena Nketia tried to express in his compositions mentioned above, some of the ideas he got while recording Ghanaian traditional music in the field. Elements used in these pieces are drum and bell rhythms, melodies from traditional as well as contemporary African music like 'highlife', and Western harmonies. In order to acquaint his students with the African rhythmic and melodic patterns used in his compositions, he wrote the booklet, *Preparatory Exercises in African Rhythm* (1963) as material for their study and practice.

When Dr. Kwame Nkrumah, Ghana's first President (1960-1966) inaugurated the Institute of African Studies at the University of Ghana he advised its academics and researchers to establish relations with European, African-American and African-Caribbean scholars outside Ghana "in order to stimulate cross-fertilization of ideas and exchange of materials on topics of common interest". (DjeDje and Carter, 1989:13). Following the President's advice, Kwabena Nketia occasionally invited African-American scholars of the performing arts, especially music, dance and drama to teach or visit the Institute. He also established links with the Institute of Jamaica, whose director, Neville Dawes, visited the University of Ghana. Among the African-Americans who honoured Nketia's invitation to the Institute of African Studies or the School of Music, Dance and Drama were the novelist and poet, Maya Angelou, the musicologist, Eileen Southern and William Carter of the Music Department at UCLA, who taught piano and musicology at the school of Music, Dance and Drama and took advantage of his presence in the country to specialise in the music of the Ashanti of Ghana.

Other scholars as well as postgraduate students from the western world also visited the Institute to gain experience in fieldwork research or work with the drummers, musicians, dancers and students of the institution. For instance, Mantle Hood, with whom Nketia had "a delightful two weeks" when he visited UCLA in 1958 (DjeDje and Carter, 1989:10), was visiting Professor at the school of Music, Dance and Drama from 1963 to 1964, and with the help of diploma students of the Institute, made a film, *Atumpan* (talking drums) during his sojourn in Ghana. Klaus Wachsmann, a renowed musicologist, who had done intensive research on the music and musical instruments of Uganda was another visitor to the Nketia programme. He expressed interest in the traditional musical instruments of northern Ghana and, accompanied by students of the Institute, went there to see how such instruments were made as well as used in performances of music and dance.

Not all the foreign musicians and academics who visited the Institute of African Studies or the School of Music, Dance and Drama went there primarily to seek assistance for or do research. Some of them taught Western instrumental performance at the Music School and they came from countries like Israel and Hungary.

Elizabeth Partos, a Hungarian lady taught violin, which several students of the School studied. She also wrote a violin tutor in the late 1960s which students used for many years. Her daughter, Judith Dhomanyi,[10] a competent cellist, also taught cello at the school.

Nketia's desire to share knowledge and experience with American, European, African-American and Africans-in-the-diaspora musicians and academics made the Institute of African Studies a centre for international scholarship in African music, history and culture. This enabled the Institute to host the sixteenth annual conference of the International Folk Music Council held in 1996. Nketia (1986:53) writes:

> This event signified not only Africa's readiness to participate in international scholarship in music but also the recognition by the wider world of the need for change in orientation that would broaden the international dimension of musicology and facilitate intercultural dialogue and communication. The experience was certainly rewarding because it was the first time that the International Folk Music Council had met outside Europe and America.

The Institute also hosted several American and European study groups from institutions of higher learning that came to hold summer or special sessions on African music and culture in Ghana.

Apart from receiving distinguished foreign visiting academics and scholars in Ghana, Kwabena

Nketia, through his active participation in international conferences relating to music, education and culture held abroad, had the opportunity to meet such personalities. Among the famous musicians, composers and music educators he met in Europe and elsewhere were: Yehudi Menuhin, the violin virtuoso and teacher; the composers, Luigi Dallapicola and Dmitri Kabalevsky; and two of the most influential music educators of the twentieth century, Zoltan Kodaly and Carl Orff. These distinguished persons were interested in Nketia's research on African music and his contribution to music education in Africa.

Kwabena Nketia's high international standing as a scholar and music educator during his Legon years resulted in his election to the executive boards of several professional or learned bodies. He was a member of the Executive Board of the International Folk Music Council from 1959 - 1970 and also served on the Board of Directors of the International Society for Music Education from 1967-1974. In 1972, he was elected First Vice-President of the Society for Ethnomusicology. The high positions he held in such societies provided the opportunity for him to give keynote address at several international conferences.

On the continent of Africa, Kwabena Nketia served as Chairman of the African Regional Secretariat of the International Music Council from 1972 to the late 1980s. He held this post concurrently with the chairmanship of the African Music Rostrum organised in cooperation with the Union of African National Radio and Television Organisation, (URTNA - French acronym), and successfully steered the affairs of the Rostrum which met biennially at the General Assembly of URTNA (held in different African countries)[11] to listen to tape recordings of music submitted by African radio stations. A selection of suitable recordings for broadcast by radio stations and organisations in Africa and other parts of the world was made at such meetings.

One would have thought that Kwabena Nketia's heavy schedule resulting from his involvement in the activities of international professional associations or learned societies during his Legon years would leave him little or no time for his research and scholarly work. On the contrary, the situation in which he found himself urged him to do more research, the findings of which he could share with other members of such organisations. He continued to write many more papers (on methodology and theoretical issues in the fields of ethnomusicology and music education) some of which were read at international seminars and conferences and were published in the journals of the associations/ societies of which he was a member. Among these are articles such as "Music Education in African Schools : A Review of the Position in Ghana" (1966); "The Place of Authentic Folk Music in Education" (1967); "The Place of Traditional Music in the Musical Life of Ghana" (1967); and "Music Education in Africa and the West : We Can Learn From Each Other" (1970) which deal with music education. Other articles like, "The Problem of Meaning in African Music" (1962), "The Interrelations of African Music and Dance", (1965) and "Musicology and African Music: A Review of

Problems and Areas of Research" (1967) deal with ethnomusicology.

Nketia's writings at this time were not confined to international journals. Not only did he write several books and papers which were published locally but also he found time to write material for use by his students and music lovers in Ghana. Two publications in Twi (published by the Ghana Publishing Corporation): *Abofodwom* (1973) – texts of Akan hunters' songs and *Ayan* (1974) – a collection of 164 texts of Akan drum language; both based on two 'dying' traditional professions of hunting and drumming, stand as testimony to Nketia's dedication as a music educator and his attempts to preserve, promote and develop Ghanaian culture (Akrofi, 1992:44). *Music in African Cultures: A Review of the Meaning and Significance of Traditional African Music* published in 1966 by the Institute of African Studies, has been used as a textbook by music students at the University. Other important 'local' publications are: *Instrumental Resources of African Music* (1969), *African Gods and Music* (1970) *The Creative Arts and the Community* (1970) and *Music of Akwapim* (1972).

Kwabena Nketia's best known book, *The Music of Africa,* was published in 1974 by W W Norton and Co. Inc. of New York, United States. This book earned him the American Society of Composers, Authors and Publishers (ASCAP) Deems Taylor Award in 1975. It has had a strong impact on the music and musical cultures in sub-Saharan Africa and has been used worldwide as a textbook for the study of African music.

A Chinese edition of the book, translated by Tang Yating was published under the title *Feizhou Yinyue* in 1982 and in 1989, a Japanese edition of it was published in Tokyo. The book has engendered such growing interest in African and African-derived music in Asia's two most influential nations, China and Japan, that DjeDje and Carter (1989:15) feel that its author, Kwabena Nketia, "might also become a bridge between Africa and Asia in our contemporary growing world of music."

For his outstanding contribution to the development of African music and culture in Ghana and the rest of the world, Kwabena Nketia was awarded the Grand Medal by the Government of Ghana in 1968 and the International Music Council – UNESCO Music Prize in 1981 for "distinguished service to music" (Nketia C.V.) 1952 through 1969 were seventeen very productive years of scholarly work in Nketia's life. He had established himself both as national and international musicologist, composer, linguist and music educator. His greatest contribution during these years was the laying of "the foundation for a programme of Ethnomusicology in Ghana from scratch." (Nketia, 1970:3)

In the 1970s two universities overseas honoured Kwabena Nketia with invitations to teach in their institutions: Harvard University in the United States appointed him Horatio Appleton Lamb Visiting Professor of Music for the Fall Semester of 1971, and from July to August 1979, he served as Visiting Professor at the University of Queensland, Brisbane, Australia.

In 1979 Kwabena Nketia gave up the directorship of the Institute of African Studies and also retired from the University of Ghana. He returned to the Department of Music, UCLA in the United States where he had, since 1969, been going every year to lecture.

CHAPTER FOUR

THE AMERICAN YEARS (1979-1992)

Kwabena Nketia spent his first three years (1979-1982) as a resident of the United States at the Department of Music and the Institute of Ethnomusicology, UCLA, where he taught full-time and also supervised the doctoral dissertations of several American and international students. According to Nketia (interview with author in July 1999), he began to put together his theoretical views on ethnomusicology towards the end of his stay at UCLA. This resulted in the writing of his paper titled "The Juncture of the Social and the Musical: The Methodology of Cultural Analysis" which he read at a conference in Berlin in 1981 and was published in *The World of Music* 23 (2) of the same year.

In 1983, Kwabena Nketia was appointed Andrew W. Mellon Professor of Music at the University of Pittsburgh, a position he held until he retired at the age of 70 in 1991. He strengthened the Ethnomusicology programme at this University and this attracted several international students to the Music Department. Among the students he taught and supervised to doctoral level, were three Africans; Damien Pwono from the Democratic Republic of the Congo, Willie Anku from Ghana and Patricia Opondo from Kenya, all of whom are now competent academics and administrators.

While at the University of Pittsburgh, Nketia did some research on the musical life of the people of the city of Pittsburgh. Writing about this, LeComte (1992:48) states:

> The practice of ethnomusicology can extend to more familiar musical traditions as well. As a project, Nketia conducted a survey in which he clipped newspaper notices and articles on all varieties of musical performance in Pittsburgh – from the symphony hall to community centers and fire-houses – to get a grip on what role music plays in that society.

When he served as the invited scholar for the 1989 Fall Meeting of the Society for Ethnomusicology Southern California Chapter, Kwabena Nketia delivered a paper on his research in Pittsburgh titled "Profiles of Musical Life in Pittsburgh" which Carter (1990:x) describes as "an instance of applied ethnomusicology to the American mainstream".

As Andrew W. Mellon Professor, Kwabena Nketia was able to bring together the units of the Music Department at the University of Pittsburgh. He got on well with the composers, ethnomusicologists, music historians, and theorists of the department who elected him Chairman after his predecessor retired in 1986. When he served as Chairman of the Music Department from 1986 to 1989 changes were made in the syllabuses so that composition students could take courses in ethnomusicology and vice-versa. Thus he contributed in some measure to the interdisciplinary dimension of the music programme at the university.

In June 1988, Kwabena Nketia received an invitation from the China Conservatory of Music, Beijing to give a six weeks course on Ethnomusicology to scholars engaged in music research and research in cognate disciplines such as Ethnology and History. He decided to focus his lectures on "Modes of Enquiry and Interpretation in Ethnomusicology" and provided a four-page course outline covering topics such as "The Nature and Scope of Ethnomusicology", "Analysis and Description of a Musical Culture", "Comparative Studies of Musical Cultures", "Music and Related Arts" and "Historical Orientations in Ethnomusicology" for the course participants. While in Beijing, he seized the opportunity to visit music institutions in the city and to discuss collaboration between their research faculty and the students at the University of Pittsburgh. He succeeded in establishing links between the China Conservatory of Music and the Music Department at Pittsburgh with the former institution acting as a clearing house for exchange programmes in research projects that may be arranged with other music institutions or scholars in China.

Kwabena Nketia was able to secure a few recordings from the China Conservatory of Music, a set of 416 slides and three cassette tapes on the History of Ancient Chinese Music which he purchased from the Institute of Music Research. On his way back from

China, he stopped in Canberra, Australia from July 16 to July 24 in order to participate in the 18th Conference of the International Society for Music Education (ISME) and to give a plenary address on the topic "Exploring Intercultural Dimensions of Music in Education". The paper was well received by the conference and was published in the ISME Year Book XV in 1988.

Nketia continued his association with professional and learned societies during his tenure at the Music Department at the University of Pittsburgh. Between 1986 and 1989 he was member of the African Studies Association. He was elected an honorary member of Phi Beta Kappa by the Pennsylvania Chapter at the University of Pittsburgh on April 27, 1989 "in recognition of high attainment in liberal scholarship" (Nketia, CV). He also accepted an invitation from Harvard University to serve as a member of the Overseers' Committee to visit the Department of Music from 1989 to 1992.

Executive Board of the International Music Council, Paris, 1975. Nketia, third from left.

Kwabena Nketia always remembers and cherishes two academic honours bestowed on him in 1989 – the presentation of a *festschrift* to him at UCLA and the delivery of the Charles Seeger Memorial Lecture at Harvard. The *festschrift*, presented in two volumes titled *African Musicology: Current Trends*, reflects "the international influence and recognition of one of the world's premier humanistic scholars, ethnomusicologists, and music educators, Professor J.H. Kwabena Nketia" (Carter, 1990:ix). Both volumes contain essays by twenty-five scholars from academic institutions throughout the United States, Africa and Europe. Carter (ibid.) sees this as "ample evidence of the pervasive, deep respect and high esteem in which Nketia is held worldwide".

The *festschrift* was presented to Kwabena Nketia at a special festival which Carter (ibid., x) describes as follows :

> The *festschrift* was officially presented to Professor Nketia on October 21, 1989. On the patio adjacent to the Department of Ethnomusicology and Systematic Musicology of Schoenberg Hall, UCLA, a festive celebration with more than 200 persons in attendance was held in the tradition of the Akan afahye. Professor and Mrs. Nketia were the guests of honor and the focus for musical and dance presentations by various African ensembles and students.

On November 11, 1989 Kwabena Nketia was invited to give the Charles Seeger Memorial Lecture at the annual conference of the Society for Ethnomusicology held at Harvard University. Nketia (interview with author in July 1999) recalls that the lecture was very well attended. "The hall was packed and many people were sitting on the floor". The lecture, "Contextual Strategies of Inquiry and Systematization" was published in *Ethnomusicology* 34, 1990. Nketia (ibid) describes it as "a sort of crowning thing in my career as an ethnomusicologist in the United States", while Carter (1990:ix) sees it as a milestone in his illustrious career and "typifies Nketia in this reflective phase of his career".

After his retirement from the University of Pittsburgh, Kwabena Nketia accepted an appointment at Kansas University as Langston Hughes Professor of African and African-American Studies for the spring semester of 1992. He said in an interview on the campus of Kansas University :

> I remember in the '50s and early '60s on my visits to institutions (in the United States) the faculty would apologize for not having ethnomusicology, because attitudes of bigotry would not allow it at the time. There were also not that many ethnomusicologists to go around. Now we have institutions turning out competent ethnomusicologists. Even Harvard is seeking an ethnomusicologist now. (Le Comte, 1992:48)

Nketia also said that African music had become a popular subject on American campuses because of its strong links with United States music forms such as jazz and pop. Those links first brought him to study and teach in the United States.

At Kansas University, Kwabena Nketia taught two African and African-American studies courses – "Structures in African Music" and "Music in African Cultures". He stressed in his class that African music required more than drums and he used the voice and African instruments like xylophones and flutes to demonstrate the diversity of the music of Africa.

When he was asked why he spent many years teaching in the United States, Kwabena Nketia answered that he thought of America as being an outpost of African music through the transformation the black culture had undergone in the country. He says :

> Teaching in the U.S.A. gave me the opportunity to look at Africa from outside and motivated me to write *The Music of Africa*, which is more or less a reflection of the results of my field research and thoughts on issues and my interests in the environment in which I worked. (Le Comte, 1992:48)

Kwabena Nketia (interview with author in July 1999) describes his one-semester stay at Kansas University as a transitional period for his return to Ghana. He wrote his proposal for the establishment of an international centre for the study of African music and dance during this period. According to him, something interesting also happened at this time. He met Judy Mitoma, a lady from UCLA, who was on attachment (as an intern) to the Rockefeller Foundation. She was interested in developing something to bring African music into focus and expressed interest in Nketia's proposal. She persuaded her director at Rockefeller Foundation to go and see Africa and with the help of Nketia, she and her director spent three days at the University of Ghana, Legon and also visited Kumasi. Nketia made a special trip to meet them in Ghana and to show them around. On his return to the U.S. to complete his term at Kansas University, Nketia pursued his proposal and sent it to the Director of the Rockefeller Foundation who recommended that a conference be organised and held at the Rockefeller Study and Conference Centre in Bellagio, Italy to examine and make appropriate recommendations to the Foundation. She provided 30,000 U.S. dollars for Nketia to organise an international conference on the theme "The Study of African Music and Dance: Problems and Prospects".

Judy Mitoma's internship at the Rockefeller Foundation came to an end before the conference could take place. Her position was taken by Damien Pwono, who had completed his Ph.D in Music at the University of Pittsburgh and who was running his own programmes for "culture and development," which brought cultural officers from Africa to Pittsburgh to learn arts management and so on. He, therefore, helped

Nketia in the organisation of the conference in Bellagio. They sent notices to people to write papers for the conference and received a large collection of papers which were circulated in advance so that the conference itself could be devoted to the discussion of the issues and problems raised in the papers.

The Rockefeller Foundation invited the Ford Foundation and the Swedish International Development Authority (SIDA) to the conference held from October 12 to 16, 1992 and at the end, they all decided that the centre should be established. The consensus was that the primary mission of the International Centre for African Music and Dance (ICAMD) "must be the promotion of international scholarship and creativity in African music and dance. It should cater for the needs of Africa as well as those of scholars, research students and creative artists world-wide" (ICAMD Newsletter, 1998:4). Kwabena Nketia, therefore, left for Ghana to set up the new centre at the University of Ghana.

CHAPTER FIVE

NKETIA'S RETURN TO GHANA : A PERIOD OF REFLECTION (1992-)

On his return to his country, Ghana, Kwabena Nketia was preoccupied with the establishment of the International Centre for African Music and Dance (ICAMD) on the premises of the University of Ghana where he held his first appointment some forty years ago. Before Christmas in 1992, Rockefeller Foundation provided a grant of US$100,000 and Ford Foundation also gave US$100,000 for the establishment of the centre. Ford Foundation was concerned about the governance and autonomy of the centre and provided an additional US$50,000 dollars for the institution of an International Advisory Board for the Centre. SIDA waited until 1995 before providing a grant for a Fellowship Programme for scholars and artists from other African countries to spend one or two semesters to work on projects at the centre. Such Fellows usually took advantage of their residency in Ghana to enrol simultaneously in the Music Department of the School of Performing Arts[12] and the Institute of African Studies for postgraduate or diploma courses related to what they were working on at the Centre.

In order to have the Centre formally established at the University of Ghana, Kwabena Nketia sent his proposal to the Academic Board of the University and it was approved. His problem at the initial stages of setting up the Centre was where it could be located. As

Emeritus Professor of the University of Ghana, a position he was appointed to in 1990, he was entitled to an office on the campus of the university. He was given a small office in the Department of Communication Studies. Since the grants he received for establishing the Centre were not meant for the construction of permanent structures, he had to look for accommodation in a department with programmes related to music and culture. He first approached the Institute of African Studies but its director was not prepared to help him because he did not like the idea of having two Directors (with Nketia as director of the Centre) in his unit. He finally went to the School of Performing Arts where the director, Professor Kofi Anyidoho and the Head of the Music Department, Dr Asante Darkwa, realising the advantage the Centre could give the school, welcomed him. He was given a small office near Dr Darkwa's office and was later provided with accommodation by Dr Darkwa to establish ICAMD.

In January 1993, Kwabena Nketia was able to establish the International Centre for African Music and Dance and serve as its founding Director. Asked why he decided to establish the Centre in Ghana he replied, "I wanted the centre of gravity of African music to be in Africa itself" (interview with author in July 1999). He explained that all the facilities for the study of African music seemed to be in the United States and he did not see why Africa itself should not provide such facilities. In his words, the objectives of the Centre are: "To raise the level of musicology and related disciplines in Africa. To attract scholars from abroad to

Africa". (ibid.) Nketia (see Vieta, 1999:450) also said :

> The need for a centre for the preservation, promotion, and scholarly study of African music and dance has long been felt by those concerned about the future of the arts as well as by scholars committed to the development of a cross-cultural view of music and dance in Africa. The centre at the University of Ghana would initiate concerted programmes that would draw on the rich resources of Africa for stimulating creativity and education in African music and dance on the continent and filling in "gaps" in our present knowledge.

The Centre operates as a semi-autonomous unit within the School of Performing Arts which has separate departments for music, dance, drama and theatre studies. It is governed by an International Advisory Board consisting of one representative from each of the major regions of Africa, one representative each of Europe, Asia, Latin America and the Caribbean and three US members (ICAMD flyer n.d.). As Director of the Centre, Kwabena Nketia is responsible for its day-to-day running. His administrative duties include making staff appointments and disbursing finances through the Registrar and Finance Office respectively of the University of Ghana. His greatest administrative achievement has been the creation of a network of regional Secretariats of ICAMD worldwide to act as "focal reference points for scholars interested in

African music and research" (interview with author in July 1999). At present there is a Secretariat at the University of Michigan, Ann Arbor, U.S. A proposal by the late Professor Khabi Mngoma, the renowned South African musicologist and music educator, and an ICAMD Board member, to set up a South African Chapter was endorsed at the 13th South African Ethnomusicology Conference held at the University of Zululand in November 1995. However, no such chapter or Secretariat had been established in South Africa by 1999. During a National Music Supervisors' Workshop held at the University of the Witwatersrand, Johannesburg from July 11-14, 1999, also attended by international scholars including Kwabena Nketia, the author asked him to set up a Regional Secretariat of ICAMD at the University of Transkei. With the consent of Professor Caesar Ndlovu, an ethnomusicologist and Head of the Department of Music Education and the University Management, a South African Secretariat of ICAMD was established within the Music Department of the University of Transkei, Umtata in May 2000. Arrangements are underway for the establishment of such Secretariats in Kenya and at the Institute of African Studies at the University of Ibadan, Nigeria. Regional Secretariats of the Centre are needed "to create a wider interest in the mission and objectives of ICAMD beyond its physical location and also ensure that its international dimension is kept constantly in view…" (ICAMD Newsletter, 1998:5).

Kwabena Nketia has also used ICAMD to establish linkages with institutions in Africa and elsewhere. A successful linkage programme brings students in Nigerian universities specialising in ethnomusicology and other disciplines of music to ICAMD for short periods to familiarise themselves with its programmes, archival and library resources. The first of these visits took thirteen postgraduate students and one lecturer from the Institute of African Studies at the University of Ibadan to the Centre from November 18 to 29, 1997. The programme consisting of lectures, seminars, performances and library and archival research was organised and coordinated by a Senior Fellow of the Centre (ICAMD Newsletter, 1998:5).

ICAMD, through Nketia's initiative, has established working relations with institutions and organisations such as the British Sound Archive, the International Music Council (UNESCO), the Centre for World Music in Holland, the Centre for Black Music Research (CBMR) Columbia College, Chicago, U.S. and St. Louis African Chorus, U.S. which is developing a resource centre for African vocal music and selected traditional performances as well as an exchange programme with the Centre. Other institutions in the U.S. which have such relations with the Centre are: the Dance Department of Swarthmore College, where a video archive of African dance forms is being developed, and where Nketia gave lectures in April, 1993 and also served as Cornell Professor in 1995; and the World Music Centre at the University of West Virginia (WVU) at Morgantown that sent annually between 1994 and 1999, American students, musicians and educators interested in American music and dance to take summer courses in these disciplines at ICAMD and the School of Performing Arts, University of Ghana, Legon.

To enable ICAMD to enrich its programme through intercultural activities, Kwabena Nketia, Fellows and Associates of the Centre, have, since 1996, honoured invitations to over a dozen international conferences and meetings held in countries like South Africa, Tanzania, Malawi, USA and Togo. Topics dealt with at such gatherings included "Pan African Festival of Art and Culture"; "Arab and Oriental Influences on African Traditional Music and Dance"; "Preparation of Primary School African Music Teaching Manuals"; and "Cultural Policies for Development". (See ICAMD Newsletter, 1998: 18-19)

In order to fulfil its mission, ICAMD regularly hosts national and international conferences and workshops geared towards the promotion of research and performance activities in African music and dance as well as the provision of opportunities for academics and artists from Africa and the Diaspora to meet and discuss matters of mutual interest. Such conferences and workshops, held between 1993 and 1998 are listed in the ICAMD Newsletter, 1998 (pp10-11). The themes of such gatherings included: "Intercultural Dimensions of African Music and Dance"; "African Composer's Forum and Workshop"; "Music and Healing in Africa and the Diaspora"; and "African Church Music".

Another activity Kwabena Nketia has managed to organise successfully at ICAMD is the institution of Memorial Lectures that honour outstanding African musical personalities. The Fela Sowande Memorial Lecture was inaugurated at the University of Ibadan, Nigeria in 1996, and a Memorial Lecture for Ephraim Amu of Ghana was inaugurated in cooperation with the National Theatre and the Arts Critics and Reviewers Association of Ghana (ACRAG) on May 26, 1998 at the National Theatre in Accra under the auspices of the Ghana Academy of Arts and Sciences (ICAMD Newsletter, 1998:12). On January 18, 2000 the Ephraim Amu Memorial Lecture was delivered by Professor Kofi Agawu,[13] the outstanding Ghanaian musicologist and theorist currently teaching at Princeton University in the United States. He began his lecture titled "The Legacy of Ephraim Amu" with an acknowledgement of the International Centre for African Music and Dance for its part in organising the event. He said:

> I pay particular tribute to the Centre's Director, Professor Kwabena Nketia. All of us who study African music are much indebted to Professor Nketia, for there is hardly a topic on which he has not written: funeral dirges, surrogate languages of Africa, the compositional process, aesthetic issues, music in development, modern African music, even African pianism, among many others. How much poorer the field would be without his contributions. (Agawu, 2000:1).

Memorial Lectures planned for the immediate future are: the Nicholas George Ballanta Memorial Lecture in Sierra Leone and the Reuben T. Caluza Memorial Lecture in South Africa.

As part of its mission to promote African music and dance, ICAMD maintains and trains a Resident Artists group, Hewale Sounds, an instrumental ensemble of African music. The group was formally inaugurated at the Centre for National Culture, Accra on February 3, 1996. Its members conduct workshops and give performances of traditional and modern compositions arranged for indigenous instruments. The group is also involved in ICAMD's outreach programmes for schools. In July 1998, it travelled to South Africa at the invitation of the Organizing Committee of the 25th Annual Conference of the International Society of Music Education (ISME) held in Pretoria to perform Ghanaian music and introduce the international community to Ghanaian traditional instruments such as *seperewa, atenteben, gonje* and *gome*. At the instance of the author, the group visited South Africa again in November/December 1999 to participate in the International Festival of Folk Arts and Culture held in Umtata, from December 5 to 12, 1999. The Hewale Sounds, which operates under the directorship of Kwabena Nketia and Clemence Adom, a Research Fellow at ICAMD and Artistic Director of the group, has also performed in Cote d'Ivoire, Norway, the United States of America and Jordan.

Kwabena Nketia has appointed some of the academics and researchers he worked with during the period he served as Director of the Institute of African Studies and the School of Music, Dance and Drama to the staff of ICAMD. Among them are : the late octogenarian, A.M. Opoku with whom he built the Ghana

Dance Ensemble in the 1960s, who was a Programme Associate for dance; S. D. Asiama, an ethnomusicologist at the Institute of African Studies, who is also a Programme Associate for the Church Music Institute; Asante Darkwa of the Music Department, School of Performing Arts, who serves concurrently as Acting Director and Programme Associate for the Church Music Institute of ICAMD and Gustav O. Twerefoo, a former Head of the Department of Music, University of Venda, South Africa, who is a consultant and Programme Associate for music education. Because of his interdisciplinary background and his strong belief in sharing knowledge and experience with other people, Kwabena Nketia is able to relate to the work as well as the research projects of these Programme Associates.

ICAMD has overgrown the space currently allocated to it in the Music Department of the School of Performing Arts, University of Ghana, and is in dire need of new structures to accommodate its expanded programmes. Hence Kwabena Nketia's present desire to have a new building constructed for the Centre.

Kwabena Nketia has not confined his activities to the running of ICAMD. He has been actively involved in academia and the development of arts and culture in Ghana since he returned to his home country in 1992. He teaches two courses for upper level bachelor's as well as master's and doctoral students in the Music Department at the School of Performing Arts. The first course, "Compositional Techniques in African Music" has two phases – a traditional music component and another for contemporary music. The second course is titled "Theories and Methods in Ethnomusicology". Nketia (interview with author in July 1999) said he would give up teaching in the year 2000 in view of an increase in his volume of work at ICAMD and his international obligations but he was in the lecture room at Legon throughout 2002.

In April 1993, the University of Ghana conferred on Kwabena Nketia an honorary degree of Doctor of Letters (Hon. D. Litt), for his "immense contribution to the study of African music" which has "received world-wide acknowledgement" (Vieta, 1999:450). Nketia had earlier, in March 1993, won the highest national award in the Arts – the Entertainment Critics and Reviewers Association of Ghana (ECRAG) "Flagstar" Award- "for his great contribution to the promotion of Ghanaian Arts" (ibid.)

In national affairs Kwabena Nketia has continued to make immense contributions to the development of arts and culture in Ghana as he did from the period before Ghana's independence and through the 1960s and 1970s. He was a Foundation Fellow of the Ghana Academy of Arts and Sciences and has served as Vice-President for two terms and President of the Academy for only one term, since his external obligations prevent him from renewing his term with this august national learned society. He also served as Chairman of the Ghana National Theatre Board from 1993 to 1997.

Nketia speaking at a conference at the University of Ghana, 1997
Left to Right: Prof A.M. Opoku, Prof. Florence Dolphyne, Nketia

Kwabena Nketia has continued to write papers for delivery at conferences and public lectures. The papers he has written in the past five years include the following:

1. "National Development and the Performing Arts of Africa," 1995.

2. "Intellectual Agenda for Coping with Social Reality", a Presidential Address for the 38th Anniversary of the Ghana Academy of Arts and Sciences.

3. "The Challenge of Cultural Preservation in a Dynamic Social Environment" presented at a symposium of the Ghana National Festival of Arts NAFAC 98.

Although Kwabena Nketia describes his career since 1992 (his return to Ghana after years of teaching in the United States) as a period of reflection, it has been business as usual. He has continued to teach, publish, run a centre and travel extensively throughout the world to lecture and attend conferences. Age never seems to catch up with an octogenarian of such varied talents.

Nketia at Mampong, Asante, 1998

CHAPTER SIX

THE EDUCATIONAL VALUE OF NKETIA'S SOURCE MATERIALS

This chapter examines the educational value of Nketia's source materials, especially his books on African musicology and some of his papers on ethnomusicology and African music and culture.

6.1 Books on African Musicology

Six of Nketia's books on African musicology are discussed. They are: *Akanfoɔ Nnwom Bi* (1949), *Funeral Dirges of the Akan People* (1955), *African Music in Ghana* (1962), *Drumming in Akan Communities of Ghana* (1963), *Folk Songs of Ghana* (1963) and *The Music of Africa* (1974). All of them, except the last, are publications on the music and culture of Ghana.

6.1.1 *Akanfoɔ Nnwom Bi*

This work consists of texts of 164 Akan songs Nketia was taught by six persons : two old women and a man from his hometown, Asante Mampong, and three men at Akuapem Akropong where he taught at the Presbyterian Training College. He expresses his gratitude to these persons as well as to C.A. Akrofi, under whom he served as an assistant at the Language Bureau in the 1940s, for helping him with the presentation of the material in this publication.

Of his six books, this one is unique in that it is written entirely in Twi. There are no English translations of the texts. Also there are no music examples to help the reader know what each song sounds like. The song texts appear under headings like : *Adowa, Adenkum, Sobom* (recreational musical types); *Nnwonkorɔ, Mmobomme*[14] (female recreational music); and *Asafo* (men's warrior music). Ten of the texts (Nos. 150-160) are from instrumental music. Nketia places them under the heading *Mmɛn Nnwom* and explains in the introduction of this book that not all Akan music is sung. However pieces for instruments like *atɛntɛbɛn*, *odurugya* (end-blown flute made from the bark of cane) and *ntahera* (ivory horn) may be doubled by vocal texts. He adds that this happens at the courts of chiefs. In this book song text numbers 153-155 are performed by *ntahera*, while numbers 156-160 are performed by *odurugya*.

Another instrumental musical type mentioned in this book is Akwadum which Nketia describes as an ancient ensemble comprising *atumpan*, two small drums and *agyegyewa* (iron cymbals). Song texts 150-152 are for such an ensemble, although Nketia emphasizes that No.152 is often performed by the group with one instrument playing the text while the other instruments accompany it.

The educational value of this book is stated in the Preface in Twi:

> *Yen ani da so sɛ adwuma yi bɛkanyan afoforɔ ama wɔaboaboa yɛn nnwom a ɛreyera yi bi ano na yɛnam so ahu sɛnea nananom hyehyɛɛ won nnwom mu nsɛm ahwɛ so ayɛ bi*

In the above quotation, Nketia expresses the hope that his book will inspire the present generation, especially the youth, to learn and compile some of our songs which are becoming extinct so that they can find out how our forefathers handled the texts of their music and emulate them.

6.1.2 Funeral Dirges of the Akan People

Nketia's objectives are clearly stated in the first paragraph of the preface:

> This monograph on Akan Funeral Dirges deals principally with the dirges of the Twi (Asante, Akyem, Kwawu, Akuapem) and Fante speaking peoples of the Gold Coast. It is in two parts. Part one deals with the background of the dirges and their main features considered from linguistic, literary and musical points of view. Part Two gives sample texts of dirges in English, Twi and Fante; it is in five sections, each one illustrating some point of form or content discussed in Part One.

We learn from this book that the dirge is linked with "other social activities of the funeral such as singing, drumming and dancing, the pouring of libations and the firing of guns, all of which spring from attitudes arising from beliefs about this world and the hereafter, and from the complex of relationships binding living men to one another and to the departed." (p.131). Akan custom, therefore, requires that the singing of funeral dirges be an integral part of the funeral celebration.

Other important characteristics of the dirge which Nketia (p.132) reveals to the reader are:

> In building up dirges, some words such as personal names, kinship terms, place names and words for indicating origin and identity are pivotal and have the greatest collocability.

> The medium through which the themes, language and literary modes of the dirge are communicated is "speech combined with music", and accompanied by tears, sobs and bodily movement. The singing of the dirge is the prerogative of women.

> As a creative verbal-musical expression, the dirge takes its place alongside the poetry of songs, drums, horns and pipes.

In the light of the above, Nketia concludes that :
In studying the dirge, therefore, we have been studying ...social expressions and aspects of the culture of the Akan people (p.132).

In his review of this book, Hugh Tracey (1956:82) writes:

> Mr. J H Nketia gives an objective account of the Funeral Dirges of his own country from the point of view of one who is not only an observer, but who also shares the emotional and spiritual virtues of the occasion.

The above comment by Tracey shows that Nketia has intimate knowledge of the dirge of the Twi and Fante speaking people of his country which he shares with the reader of this book. For instance we learn from the book that one of the important elements in the celebration of an Akan funeral is the dirge which has a wealth of historic family or clan references. On this point Tracey (ibid) commends Nketia for giving an "admirable description of the social setting of the events surrounding a funeral, describing in detail the behaviour patterns which are expected of relatives and other members of the community". He adds that Nketia "extracts the poetic elements of the dirge in a manner which no one but a participant could emulate. It is perhaps in this regard that this work appears to be most significant". Again Tracey (ibid) informs us that "there are delightful touches throughout the narrative which reveal Nketia's intimate knowledge of the mourners, their little vanities and their frank enjoyment of the occasion as they unfold themselves in traditional action and conventional signs."

Some of the relevant information on the dirge culled from the narrative (see Tracey, ibid.) is as follows:

> ...the singing of the dirge (by women) is usually not an organised performance... Each singer sings dirges of her own choice, often without regard to what others may be singing or how they may be singing them.
>
> Women mourners do not stop their dirges while the funeral lasts but there is nothing to prevent them from taking a good rest from time to time.
>
> If a woman failed to sing a dirge at the funeral she would be badly criticised, and possibly suspected of having something to do with the death.
>
> A good singer wins in emotional appeal, she moves her audience ...mock-sadness is discouraged. A tear should fall, lest you are branded a witch or a callous person. If a tear is physiologically difficult to shed, you must induce it by some means; ...it would be better to have the marks of tears on your face than nothing at all.

The above information provides knowledge that can be drawn on by "scholars and educators who have to plan educational programmes and collect and arrange curricular materials for the teaching of African music" (Nketia, 1970:11). Nketia (1991:88) also says that he "found out that some literate Akan people who did not know the dirges of their clans or lineages used my work as a reference book".

6.1.3 *African Music in Ghana*

This book was published by Longmans Green and Co., London, in 1962 and also by Northwestern University Press, Evanston, in 1963. The review in this chapter is devoted to the latter publication.

This book, says Nketia (Preface vii), "is a short general introduction" to the music of Ghana. He provides for the reader a brief account of the social setting of musical activity and the occasions on which it is performed, types of music and of performing groups, vocal music, melody and harmony, and the rhythm of songs. He includes a very short survey of musical instruments and a bibliography. As this publication is intended to provide a basis for study and further investigation, Nketia (p.110-113) arranges the bibliography in five sections covering, the ethnographic background, notes and essays on Ghanaian music, song texts and drum language, collections of folk songs and original compositions and general (select bibliography). Academics, students and readers interested in the music of Ghana will find a wealth of material in the bibliography although many of the sources listed in it date back to the 1920s and 1930s and are difficult to come by.

Since this book concerns African music in Ghana,

the chapter which is of most worth to the reader, in this author's opinion, is the third, titled "Musical Types". In it, Nketia (p.10) gives a tripartite classification on a functional basis, of the musical types of Ghana as: "(1) those which are used for providing recreational music; (2) those used as "occasional" music, and (3) those used as incidental music. He clearly defines each of these categories and names specific types of music, for each of them, performed by various Ghanaian ethnic groups such as the Akan, Ga-Adangme, Ewe, Frafra, Dagomba, Builsa and Kassena-Nankani. Anticipating that the reader would have problems differentiating between the second (occasional) and third (incidental) classifications of his tripartite model, Nketia (p.14) takes pains to clear the air with the statement:

> Incidental music tends to be secondary in the framework of the whole event, while "occasional" music forms an integral part of the proceedings of a given occasion, "Occasional" music may have ritual implications. Incidental music on the other hand may have no such implications; it often lacks the seriousness of the former.

In chapter four of the book, devoted to performing groups and their music, Nketia provides four tables to illustrate the distribution of social groups or organisations which have a number of musical types in common, especially among four Ghanaian ethnic groups in Southern Ghana – Akan, Ga, Adangme and Ewe. The tables not only contain lists of musical types but also their names in the languages of the four groups mentioned above. They are very useful since they provide the reader with informative material on the music performed by occasional and popular bands such as hunters' and warrior associations, cult groups and court musicians. It is regrettable, though, that these tables do not include the musical types of the ethnic groups of Northern Ghana, mentioned in the previous chapter namely, the Frafra, Dagomba, Builsa and Kassena-Nankani.

Of the twelve chapters in this book, five of them are "technical" and therefore, suitable for music students, academics or other people interested in the serious study of Ghanaian music. They are: Chapter 6 – Form and Technique in Vocal Music; Chapter 7 – Melody; Chapter 8 - Harmony in Vocal Music; Chapter 9 – The Rhythm of Songs; and Chapter 10 – Instrumental Resources.

Writing about melody in Chapter 7 Nketia (p.34) makes the following observation:

> From the evidence of extensive recordings of Ghanaian music, it appears that the scale systems in use in Ghana are diatonic in conception and that microtones are not integral elements of melodic structure.

He identifies two kinds of diatonic scales – the pentatonic and heptatonic – which "are in common use in vocal music, and each ethnic group specialises in one of them" (p.34). However, he quickly points out that in areas of intensive cultural interaction such as the Ga area, or areas populated by immigrants of different ethnic origins such as the Gonja area, both kinds of scale are used side by side, usually in different musical types. We also learn from this chapter that varieties of the pentatonic and heptatonic scales are used by ethnic groups in both Southern and Northern Ghana. The pentatonic scale is used by the Adangme (Southern Ghana) and the Dagomba, the peoples of Wa, Mamprusi, Frafra and Kusasi (all of Northern Ghana). Then the heptatonic scale is used by the Akan (Southern Ghana) and the Builsa, the Kassena-Nankani and the Konkomba (all of Northern Ghana). Nketia describes the pentatonic scales observed in Ghana as "anhemitonic" which do not include semitones but are constructed entirely out of major seconds and minor thirds. Two arrangements of this scale in common use are C D E G A C and C D F G A C. With regard to the heptatonic scale Nketia (p.35) reveals to us that a raised fourth (F# in the scale of C) and a lowered seventh (B in the scale of C) are used occasionally in place of the natural note of the scale. He adds that such notes are best regarded as variants in melodic sequences, rather than as chromatic notes of the scale because a chromatic segment, such as F-F#-G or C-B-B has not been encountered in the melodies of Ghanaian music. On the use of raised fourths or lowered sevenths Nketia (ibid) says:

The raised fourth is somewhat rare in Akan music,...
The flattened seventh, on the other hand, is frequent and well established in Akan vocal music. Whereas a raised fourth is generally approached from the note above, the flattened seventh may be approached from a note above or below.

In the vocal music of Kassena-Nankani and Builsa, the lowered seventh does not seem to be as well established as one finds in Akan music. The raised fourth functions in two-part harmonic structures, particularly at the terminals of musical sentences which end on the fifth degree of the scale. More technical details on tonal organisation, intervals and patterns of movement, and intonation and melodic movement are provided.

As already noted, the eighth and ninth chapters of this book deal with harmony and rhythm respectively. This is what Jones (1962:116) says about these chapters:

> As to harmony, the variety of available chords and chordal sequences is surprising – though Professor Nketia in his final summary indicates that as a general rule, people – as elsewhere in Africa sing either in parallel octaves, fourths and fifths, or in parallel thirds.
>
> But what is most surprising is that the rhythmic aspects of drumming – the exhibition par excellence of African musical genius -- are dealt with in less than one page.

Jones' criticism of the chapter on rhythm may not be justified since Nketia deals with the rhythm of songs and not of drums per se in this chapter.

Nketia uses transcriptions of Ghanaian indigenous music in the seventh, eighth and ninth chapters which deal with melody, harmony and rhythm. Jones (ibid) makes negative comments about this in the following statement:

> In the transcriptions the music is all scored within conventional Western bar-lines, this, while mathematically possible, seems dynamically questionable as it appears largely to disregard the irregular melodic accents described in the text.

Jones' (ibid) review of this book also includes the following :

> While the book contains a lot of informative material, it produces a rather confused effect on the reader, owing partly to the chapter lay-out which prevents the author from handling in the same place, the various aspects of any one topic, and causes repetition, but chiefly to the literary mannerisms – the author adopts an astonishingly complicated way of saying simple things.

Jones does not have the "last word" on this book. The outstanding musicologist and scholar, Kofi Agawu (1995:2), describes Nketia's *African Music in Ghana* as "still the only comprehensive survey of music in Ghana".

6.1.4 *Drumming in Akan Communities of Ghana*

According to Nketia (p.1), this book is "restricted to a study of the social implications of Akan drumming". In the course of his intensive field research undertaken in selected Akan speaking areas of Ashanti, Kwahu, Akim Abuakwa, Akuapem and Fante in the 1950s, he was constantly reminded of the importance which the Akan people attach to the interpretation of their drumming. The drummers and other musicians with whom he worked often told him that drums "do not just play music to which one can dance : they have messages to convey in given situations" (p.2). To the Akans, therefore, drumming 'has meaning' – *'εwɔ ase'* (in Twi). Nketia (ibid) thus states:

> It is the aim of this study, therefore, to establish and illustrate the meaning which the Akan maintain underlies their drumming.

He, therefore, deals with the musical and linguistic aspects of drumming which give meaning to it.

Nketia (p.3) also informs us that 'although the Akan are divided into separate states, musically they form a homogenous group". He, however, cautions that, except where otherwise stated, the descriptions and generalisations in the book refer to the Akan area as a whole.

This book contains a wealth of material even for people who are not avid readers. The five appendices alone contain so much information that they can be used as supplementary material for a theoretical course on drumming in Ghana. For example, Appendix 1 contains twelve tables on almost everything about drumming – classification of drums, types of drums, techniques of drumming, composition of drum orchestras and so forth – Nketia discusses in all the twelve chapters of this book. Someone who is interested in ensembles of popular bands will find table 7 useful while whoever is interested in the names of state drums and types of orchestras associated with such drums may take a look at table 11. Appendix II contains the original versions of texts (Akan) quoted in the book some of which may be used by students learning speech drumming on the atumpan. Appendix III, glossary, is a useful source of reference for the drums and other musical instruments, drum pieces and dances mentioned in the book. Appendix IV contains a list of tape recordings of Akan music Nketia made in the field which may still be available at the archives of the Institute of African Studies or the International Centre for African Music and Dance, both at the University of Ghana, Legon. And finally, Appendix V is the bibliography which comprises publications produced between the 1920s and 1950s. Most of the sources listed here are Nketia's publications preceding the date of publication of this book. It is worth one's while, especially the researcher or student of Ghanaian music to read some of the references in this appendix.

Also of great value to the reader are the plates provided in the book which are photographic presentations of drums, their makers, performers of drum music, as well as drum orchestras with other instruments used in such ensembles. Plates 24 and 25, for example show the reader how drums and other instruments playing together in an orchestra appear in a musical performance.

The book also contains a list of illustrations. Figures 1 to 5 show the exterior decorations and 'eye' designs on drums such as *bɔmmaa, brɛnko, akukuadwo* and *atumpan*. These show that drums are not only musical instruments but also beautiful works of art. Figures 6 to 14 are musical illustrations used in chapters three and four on "Modes of Drumming" and "The Verbal Basis of Drumming" respectively. Figure 6 contains the rhythmic patterns of the *gong* and *bɔmmaa* drum in a piece Nketia describes as "*Bɔmmaa* prelude (Akropong)" [see p.21). People who can read music can see clearly in this figure that while the gong provides the "time line" the *bɔmmaa* drum plays not less than four different rhythmic patterns alongside it. Figure 12 is especially interesting because it contains drum beats in both note value and nonsense syllable durations. We learn from the several examples in this figure that differences in weight, pitch or rhythmic grouping of drum beats may be reflected in the sequence of nonsense syllables, for example in the choice of consonant initials. Consonants such as k, g represent heavy beats while others like t, d represent light beats. Indeed, nonsense syllables are so important in Akan drumming that Nketia (p.35) makes the following statement about them:

> Nonsense syllables then, are closely related to drum beats as ordered sounds. They have only a musical meaning and are therefore, applicable to all modes of drumming. They are part of a drummer's art and may be invented by him or by the listener, but they do not give any indication of the 'message' of instances of drumming. They show that there is a consciousness of the values of drum beats, a consciousness of the patterning, integrating and crossing of the beats of drums.

We also learn from this book that in general the Akan people use two types of drums: closed drums and open drums; the latter are more numerous and of greater importance in Akan culture than the former.

Nketia (p.171-172) identifies three modes of drumming in Akan communities: (1) The signal mode of drumming characterised by short repetitive rhythms usually played on single drums; (2) The speech mode of drumming played on a single drum, or in the case of the *atumpan* on a pair of drums. It is characterised by varied, flowing rhythms played in groups separated by pauses and generally lacking in regularity of phrasing; (3) The dance mode of drumming characterised by a regularity of phrasing or a recurrent pulse felt mentally or set by an accompanying idiophone, usually a gong *(dawuro)*.

The three modes of drumming described above are not peculiar to the Akan. According to Agawu (1995:91-92) :

> Nketia's tripartite model, which identifies a speech mode, a signal mode, and a dance mode of drumming in Akan communities, applies generally well to the Northern Ewe. Although the three modes are not equally common in Northern Ewe society – the signal mode, for example, is heard only occasionally, while the speech mode is naturally restricted by the fast dying (in some cases dead) practice of talking drums – the model facilitates a synchronic analysis of dance rhythms.

Nketia (p.5) is not unaware of the similarity of musical practice between the Akan and other ethnic groups in Ghana as can be seen in the following statement:

> The musical influence the Akan have had on other Ghanaians, on the Ga and Ewe for example, has been mainly in the use of open drums and certain kinds of songs. The Akan

atumpan and *asafo* drums, for example, are used by both Ga and Ewe, often along with the Akan texts for the drums.

Agawu (ibid,:202) concurs but remarks that although it has been three decades since the above statement was made, no study of the nature and extent of this influence has appeared. This is an area of research Ghanaian and other musicologists should try to investigate.

In addition to educating us on the modes of drumming, Nketia, (p.8) shows us the techniques of hitting the drum head:

1. hand technique – for example *apentemma* and *ɔperenten*

2. stick-and-hand technique – curved or straight stick in the right hand while the left hand is used for muting the beat of the right hand or to strike a note.

3. Stick-and-armpit control technique – for example the hour-glass drum *(donno)*

4. Stick technique – the most important for the Akan – two sticks, one in each hand for playing on a pair of drums, for example *atumpan* and *bɔmmaa*.

Since this book is devoted to the social implications of Akan drumming it is important to mention some of them, gleaned from Nketia's (p.173-174) conclusion of the book:

> In community life, social groups and organisations are responsible for drumming. They include Popular Bands, associations and the organisation of chieftaincy.
>
> Drumming plays a vital part in the meetings of warrior associations (asafo companies), for they are assembled, incited, encouraged, diverted, directed or disbanded largely by means of drumming.
>
> State drumming has the greatest variety of forms. Signal drums, talking drums and drum ensembles which play a variety of drum pieces are to be found at the courts of all leading chiefs.
>
> The drumming of all social groups, such as bands, associations and states is carried on by a few individuals appointed by common consent or by succession of office. These drummers acquire the art through social experience or more generally through formal teaching.

6.1.5 *Folk Songs of Ghana*

This book was first published by Oxford University Press in 1963. The 1973 edition, published by the Ghana Universities Press is dealt with in this review. Unlike his aforementioned books on musicology discussed in this chapter, Nketia indicates in his preface (p.x) the kinds of people for whom this book is designed: "to provide source material for performers, composers and students of African music".

He begins the introduction of this book with a brief historical account of attempts by some Ghanaians at writing some Ghanaian songs which had been practised largely by oral tradition. He cites two important publications which preceded his own: Ephraim Amu's *Twenty-five African Songs*, published in 1932 and Isaac Riverson's *Songs of the Akan People* published in 1939 and reprinted in 1954 under the title *Akan Songs;* and commends their authors for publishing "folk songs" to keep up this literacy to enable those who have acquired it to enlarge their experience of the African "idiom" at its source (p.1). Nketia (ibid) also justifies the need for these two publications and his book (reviewed here) in the following statement:

> In a rapidly changing society such as Ghana where everyone is reaching out for new forms of expression in social life as well as in music, literature and art, the study of the African heritage of "folk music" is of particular importance, for it is in this idiom that African musical values developed over the ages are enshrined.

Furthermore, he explains, also in his introduction, that he uses the term "folk song" in this publication as a convenient designation to distinguish songs in the traditional African idiom which are closely integrated with everyday life from those in the new popular and fine art traditions that have emerged in modern Ghana. The term "folk song", he asserts, "is used in this and succeeding volumes in the broad sense of music perpetuated largely by oral tradition and integrated with a living, surviving or historical pattern of community life" (p.2).

The book contains fifty-six transcribed Akan songs grouped under four musical types. Each of the four sections of its contents is devoted to one musical type: Section One: *Nnwonkorɔ*- sixteen songs; Section Two: *Asaadua* – seven songs; Section Three: *Adowa* – thirteen songs; and Section Four: *Apoɔ* – twenty songs. Each section begins with an introduction in which the social background, distinctive structural features, type of accompaniment used, manner of performance, poetry and features of movement of each musical type are discussed. Also provided in each section are transcriptions of basic clap, instrumental rhythmic, and vocal melodic patterns used in the performance of songs of the musical types. Nketia goes to the extent of providing full scores for the musical types. For example, there is a "complete score" for *Asaadua* music (p.72) which unearths the organisation of the music as follows:

...there are essentially only three main entries:

1. the entries of rattle, castanet and gong (dawuro)
2. the entries of the double gong (nnawuta), hourglass drum, medium and large frame drums; and
3. the entries of the small frame drum and "pati" drum,

Added to the above is the explanation:

> The "polyrhythmic effect" of the music is achieved through the recurrences of these staggered entries as the basis of phrasing, and the use of a basic cross rhythm of two against three.

A full score of *Adowa* music is provided (p.99) but unlike that of the *Asaadua* one described above, it is intended to give some indication of how the various entries are organized. The two examples given above are useful for literate performers of Ghanaian music who can read music, as well as composers who wish to write music in this vein.

Nketia makes several statements on his transcriptions with regard to scales, tonality, rhythm, time signatures, and accompanying musical instruments, all of which are important in the performance of the songs of the four Akan musical types he deals with. Some of these are:

> The scale used by the Akan is diatonic in

character and heptatonic in structure. Although pitch values do not correspond exactly to those of equal temperament, they are near enough to just intonation to make the use of the staff adequate for practical purposes. (p.3)

Keys in which most of the songs were sung ranged from F to B (F, G , G, A A and B) (p.3)

In spite of this statement, Nketia decided to write the transcriptions of all the songs in this book in one key, (C), irrespective of the actual keys in which they were sung when recorded.

Bar lines have been used mainly as time markers for indicating beats and not primarily as markers of melodic accents (p.4).

Conventional time signatures ($^2_4$ $^3_4$ and $^6_8$) are used for indicating the number of equal durational units found within a bar. They do not necessarily indicate stress patterns. In all the songs, the unit of measure is the crotchet or the dotted crotchet (p.4).

Where double time signatures are used, one is put into brackets. For example $^6_8$ ($^3_4$) implies that changes from groups of six quavers to groups of three crotchets will be encountered in the song (p.5). With the exception of *nnwonkorɔ* songs which may be "accompanied" by handclapping only, all the songs in this volume are "accompanied" by drums and idiophones. The accompanying rhythm played by a "gong" or by handclapping, is often a short phrase, ...repeated in the same form over and over again throughout the entire performance. In most of the scores it has been represented as a two-bar phrase. (p.7)

Songs are always performed in solo and chorus form in which the two sections frequently alternate... A common method of singing the chorus response is to sing in two parts moving in parallel thirds.

All the above information will, hopefully, help the people for whom the book is written, to digest the invaluable material it contains.

Of great value in the book are the eleven preparatory exercises appearing on pages 11 through 15. Nketia explains that they have been "devised to give musicians approaching African rhythm for the first time and those accustomed to other methods of writing African music practice in handling African rhythms or interpreting the notation used here before tackling the songs." He advises such musicians to emulate the African who learns to play rhythms in patterns. These rhythms should, therefore, be learnt in unit groups and patterns and steady metronomic beats should be adhered to.

6.1.6 *The Music of Africa*

This is the only one of the six books discussed in this chapter which deals with the music of the continent of Africa rather than the music of Ghana or its majority Akan people. It has been designed as "an introduction to the music of Africa for the general reader and the college student". It also provides a broad survey of the musical traditions of Africa with respect to their historical, social, and cultural backgrounds, as well as an approach to musical organisation, musical practice, and significant aspects of style" (preface, xi).

Teaching in the United States of America motivated Nketia to write this book. He, therefore, expresses his gratitude to those who encouraged him to write it or gave him the opportunity to work on parts of it by inviting him to write or lecture on aspects of the music of Africa. He mentions in particular the Department of Music and Institute of Ethnomusicology, University of California at Los Angeles, where he taught for fifteen years, the Music Department of Harvard University, where he lectured for a semester as the Horatio Appleton Lamb Visiting Professor of Music in 1971. He also mentions Nissio Fiagbedzi, a colleague at the University of Ghana, who transcribed the Ewe texts.

The contents of the book are organised in four sections each with a heading as follows:

Section One -	The Social and Cultural Background
Section Two –	Musical Instruments
Section Three –	Structures in African Music
Section Four -	Music and Related Arts.

There are also three appendices each devoted to selected discography, location of ethnic groups mentioned in the text, and African terms used in the text. The Bibliography includes four of Nketia's books discussed in this chapter namely *Funeral Dirges of the Akan People, African Music in Ghana, Drumming in Akan Communities of Ghana,* and *Folk Songs of Ghana.* The book is also illustrated with music examples and photographs as well as maps to help readers unfamiliar with the ethnic groups and countries of Africa.

As mentioned in Chapter Three (p.47) of this biographical study, Nketia's *The Music of Africa,* has been used worldwide as a textbook for the study of African music to such an extent that it has been translated into German, Italian, Chinese and Japanese. Agawu (1995:2) aptly describes it as Nketia's "widely used textbook".

6.2 *Papers on Ethnomusicology and African Music and Culture*

Nketia's papers which fall under the above category number about a hundred. However, only the following ten, which I consider to be the most important, will be discussed in this chapter:

> *The Problem of Meaning in African Music (1962)*
> *Ethnomusicology in Ghana (1970)*
> *The Juncture of the Social and the Musical :*

The Methodology of Cultural Analysis (1981)
The Aesthetic Dimension in Ethnomusicological Studies (1984)
African Music and Western Praxis: A Review of Western Perspectives on African Musicology (1986)
Contexual Strategies of Inquiry and Systematization (1990)
Music and Cultural Policy in Contemporary Africa (1991)
National Development and the Performing Arts of Africa (1995)
The Challenge of Cultural Preservation in a Dynamic Social Environment (1998)
Intellectual Agenda for Coping with Social Reality (n.d)

6.2.1 The Problem of Meaning in African Music

This short, seven-page paper is Nketia's first philosophical exposé on the concept of "meaning". It should be noted that, at the time it was written, he had published four of his six books mentioned earlier in this chapter, in each of which he showed the importance of meaning in the music of Ghana. We can recall that in his fourth book, *Drumming in Akan Communities of Ghana* (p.2) the drummers and musicians he worked with drew his attention to the fact that drumming 'has meaning' – εwɔ ase (in Twi). Nketia begins this paper with the assertion :

The study of music as a universal aspect of human behaviour is becoming increasingly recognised as the focus of Ethnomusicology. (p.1).

Although he cites several scholars in his discussion with regard to ethnomusicology and the vital role it plays in the meaning of the music of mankind, he is very much influenced by two sources: 1) Seeger (1952:366) who said that the ultimate task of musicology "is to contribute to the study of man what can be known of man as music maker and music user," and 2) Merriam (1959,1960) who defines ethnomusicology as "the study of music in culture". Nketia disagrees with some scholars who sometimes say that the African cannot talk about his music and he gives as an example Jones' (1954:26) statement that, "No African can sing you his scale as he is not aware that he has one" (see p.1). "On the contrary", he argues, "the African is interested in what he does and derives pleasure from it even in ritual situations" (p.2). With reference to his work among the Akan people of Ghana, Nketia informs us that he was constantly made aware of the fact that there were other "areas of meaning" besides the sounds of drums and voices. Indeed, he found that the musical tradition of the Akan did not consist only of repertoire but also of a body of knowledge in terms of which music took place or was interpreted. He also observed that often references to music emphasised it as an event, and also as a process in time. The Akans also had ways of quoting rhythm patterns or imitating drum rhythms when they had to talk about these or when in the course of the narration of a folktale one had to imitate verbally what some drums played.

Nketia avers that whereas the analysis of scales, modes, melodic direction, intervals, harmony and so on provides one type of meaning to those accustomed to thinking of music in those terms, "to the African performer and his collaborators and "listeners", the music means much more than these, for it is part of a way of life". (p.3). It is evident from his discussion that in the field of African music, the ethnomusicologist must be cognizant of 'culture' in the material he handles. Hence Nketia affirms that "The study of music in culture is not only desirable but necessary" (p.4)

Nketia (p.4) recommends the 'contextual' technique for dealing with aspects of meaning in synchronic studies of African music. In his experience such a technique as has been used in the analysis of linguistic and ethnographic data handles "music in culture" most adequately. The 'contexual' approach is thus implicit in the definition 'music in culture', culture being the context in which music is studied.

We also learn from this paper that in synchronic studies of African music there is the need for paying attention to the processes that shape and define 'music in culture'. Since African music is regarded as an event occurring in varied contexts of situation, the researcher should try to analyse such event and the components of its context from the point of view of the immediate situation he observes and the situation in a general context of culture.

In the first instance Nketia advises the researcher to observe;

(i) the participants - musicians, dancers and others
(ii) relevant actions such as dance movements and other actions occurring simultaneously with the music,
(iii) relevant objects such as musical instruments, sound producing objects such as dancers idiophonic adornment and so on, not regarded as 'instrument' in the culture or outside the dance situation,
(iv) the music considered in terms of (i) – (iii) and in terms of established categories of musicological analysis, including the analysis of song texts.

In the second instance the researcher should study musical events in respect to (v) the body of culturally defined usage that govern them, including the examination of different occasions of performance and the values in terms of which they take place, (vi) the relationship of musical events with other aspects of culture, and (vii) factors which affect the course of musical practice such as culture contact or social change.

In light of the above Nketia (p.5) makes the following statement:

> Meaning in African music then must be regarded not as involving one statement but a plurality of statements derived from different but mutually related phases of investigation of ethnographic and musical character, and one might more appropriately speak of the areas, or modes of meaning rather than meaning in general.

Other aspects of meaning, according to him, are expressed in statements dealing with the interrelations of structure and function, structure and context, structure and movement or dancing, while the relationship between music and other aspects of culture provide yet another mode or modes of meaning.

In conclusion, Nketia (p.6) remarks that a contextual technique such as he has outlined in this paper "enables the various modes of meaning in African music to be investigated and stated in a comprehensive manner without losing sight of 'music in culture' or of our ultimate task of contributing to the study of man "what can be known of man as music maker and music user".

6.2.2 *Ethnomusicology in Ghana*

Although he was promoted to full professorial rank at the University of Ghana in 1963, it was not until six years later, on November 20, 1969 that Nketia delivered this paper for his Inaugural Lecture. The paper is a review of the seventeen years of work that he had done at the University in which he had to lay the foundations for a programme of ethnomusicology in his country, Ghana.

We are made aware of the focus of his ethnomusicology programme with the statement:

> The general area in ethnomusicology which has been our concern in Ghana is non-Western music and the music of Africa has been our field of specialisation within this area. (p.3)

Some of the points of view Nketia expressed in his earlier writings are echoed in this paper. For instance, his statement:

> Ethnomusicology now lays emphasis on the study of 'music in culture' as well as the study of the music of every culture 'in terms of itself' and 'in terms of its cultural context' (p.5)

reminds us of what he tried to say about the essence of ethnomusicology in his paper, *The Problem of Meaning in African Music* discussed in 6.2.1 above.

One gets the impression, from reading this paper, that the importance of ethnomusicology in the promotion of African music in Ghana cannot be overemphasized.

The following statement confirms this opinion:

Apart from being an interesting academic discipline, ethnomusicology has an important task, indeed an important mission in Ghana - that of providing a body of musical knowledge that can be drawn on as much by artists – composers, performers, dancers, producers – as by scholars and educators who have to plan educational programmes and collect and arrange curricular materials for the teaching of African music. It is to ethnomusicology that we have to look for a systematic theory of African music that will reflect the basic principles that underlie traditional musical practice. (p.11)

We should be concerned with four levels of interest in our efforts to establish a successful programme of ethnomusicology in Ghana. Nketia's mention and discussion of these levels (p.11-22) are summarised below :-

1. The scholarly level of interest

This needs considerable emphasis on fieldwork because the existing bibliographical material on the music of Ghana before 1952, when Nketia started his programme, was hopelessly inadequate. Also previous sources had been prepared by Western observers who had musical interests but who had had no preparation for this kind of study. In spite of the unfavourable comments which some of these writers made about African musical practices, they provide useful data where their accounts are factual and purely descriptive, data which can be used in historical studies.

Although the scholarly study of music is the primary concern of ethnomusicology, our research must be related to problems of immediate interest to Ghana and it should contribute first and foremost to the development of music and the performing arts in Ghana. In other words, we must link ethnomusicology – a research discipline – to music studies.

2. The 'artistic' interest

At this level the Nketia programme tried to build on Amu's pioneering, creative approach to African musical studies. Training himself in African music in the 1920s by learning traditional songs, *atɛntɛbɛn* and *odurugya* flute music and the music of the Akan *seperewa* (harp-lute), Amu tried to discover the essential character of the music of his own people and the resources that he could use creatively. This process has been continued through the creative use of such material in composition as well as in performance programmes evident in the activities of the School of Music, Dance and Drama and the Ghana Dance Ensemble both of which Nketia established at the University of Ghana in the early 1960s The 'artistic' level involves the preservation of the arts of Ghana not only by studying them in a scholarly fashion and writing about them but also by keeping them alive in performance programmes. Hence the Research Fellows of the Institute of African Studies who worked with Nketia included not only scholars interested in academic research but also composers and choreographers who could demonstrate their research in practical terms.

3. *A link between Ethnomusicology and the field of Music Education.*

This level can be achieved through research in music education as well as the development of African materials in music courses. The programmes of the School of Music, Dance and Drama were designed with this in mind. However training in both African and Western musics described as "bimusicality" was encouraged.

To fulfil this level of interest, basic research projects in music education such as investigations into the musical background of the school child and the music of his community have been conducted in various areas of Ghana.

4. *The popular level of interest*

This was to fulfil the interest of academic communities in Ghana and abroad, school children and adult communities interested in knowing about traditional Ghanaian or African music, in listening to and watching performances of music and dance and related arts of Africa.

The dissemination of information acquired through ethnomusicological research on a more popular level, for instance, led to the formation, in 1958, of the Ghana Music Society which was a forum for sharing experiences with music lovers and for stimulating general interest in the development of music in Ghana. In fulfilment of the popular level of interest, the Nketia programme has shared the fruits of its work with other members of the community through publications, performances of the Ghana Dance Ensemble and other groups in the Institute of African Studies connected with research and teaching programmes.

The popular level of interest also encouraged the Nketia programme to vigorously plan and implement cross-cultural studies in order to link its work with those of the Americas and the Caribbean in the field of African and African-derived music. This, as mentioned in chapter three (p.43) of this biographical study, made the Institute of African Studies a base for international scholarship in African music, history and culture.

Conclusion

This paper gives us food for thought as far as the development of research in African music and culture in Ghana is concerned. Nketia concludes it with the statement:

> I am happy, therefore, to have had this first public opportunity to speak about Ethnomusicology in Ghana, ...it is my hope that I have been able to share with you my conception of this field of study and its practical implications

in the context of present day Ghana and the new 20th century world of music.

The above statement nothwithstanding, I consider this paper as Nketia's valedictory speech to the University of Ghana although it was made ten years prior to his retirement from this institution in 1979.

6.2.3 *The Juncture of the Social and the Musical : The Methodology of Cultural Analysis*

As mentioned in chapter four (p.4) of this biographical study, Nketia had begun to put together his theoretical views on ethnomusicology towards the end of his tenure at the University of California at Los Angeles, and this resulted in the writing of this paper.

He expresses concern that ethnomusicologists had forgotten that the central subject of their discipline was music as their attitudes to music had become ambivalent in their search for an appropriate methodology for the cultural analysis of music. He says :

> There seems to be a shift of focus from investigation into 'meaning' in music viewed in terms of the musical experience to considerations of 'meaning' in terms of general culture, whereas they should be complementary and not mutually exclusive. (p.22)

Nketia, therefore, suggests and discusses four approaches to guide ethnomusicologists as they search for a meaningful application of the concept of culture to the study of music. These are :

1) the cultural theme approach;
2) the causal relations approach;
3) the contextual approach, and
4) the cultural factor approach.

He points out though that our exploration should not be limited to these four approaches since "methodologies are dictated by goals of research and problems to be investigated" (p.33).

His conclusions are as follows :

Of the four approaches, the thematic and the causal contribute little to our understanding of music as an aural experience, since their primary goal is the understanding of general culture. However, they could be invaluable in the study of music as a social or cultural experience and in specific fields such as music and social change. (p.33)

As a holistic approach the contextual approach has great value in descriptive studies but it is inadequate when it comes to interpretation. Similarly the cultural factor approach may over-emphasize abstraction and could very well be over-interpretive. A combination of the contextual and cultural factor approaches might therefore prove more adequate for handling problems of meaning in music. To this end the musical culture concept should be given greater attention as the focus of ethnomusicology. (p.34)

The concept of musical culture does not exclude music from the concept of culture... It should therefore enable us to integrate the social and the musical through a unitary field theory... and the development of a methodology of cultural analysis that takes us beyond stylistic analysis to wider problems of meaning in music, a methodology that reflects the concerns of musicians in search of understanding of music as a particular sphere of cultural activity. (p.34-35)

This paper addresses a wider audience – ethnomusicologists worldwide. Unlike the two (preceding) papers discussed earlier there are not many specific references to Africa, although there is a picture of two Senufo flute players from the Ivory Coast in West Africa (see p.29). In other words, the four approaches propounded by Nketia serve the needs of ethnomusicologists from all cultures who are interested in music as a "sphere of cultural activity".

6.2.4 *The Aesthetic Dimension in Ethnomusicological Studies*

This paper is concerned with aesthetics, a branch of philosophy. "The need for ethnomusicological approaches to the study of the aesthetic dimension of music", says Nketia, " has long been recognized, for aesthetic principles, ideas, values and behaviour are developed in the context of society and culture and are related not only to the types of music each society or social group cultivates, but also to its value system, concept of reality, and the fundamental needs or goals it seeks to fulfil through music". (p.3)

This apt statement is followed by a brief discussion of the views of scholars like Mantle Hood and Manfred Bukofzer after which Nketia opines that "aesthetics of music must concern itself not only with enquiry in general philosophical terms, but also with empirical studies of aesthetic principles in the variety of musical expressions in oral and written traditions cultivated in different regions of the world". (p.4)

But aesthetics is not without problems. We learn from Nketia's review of the present state of aesthetics in ethnomusicological studies that a number of difficulties have retarded progress in the systematic study of aesthetics in ethnomusicological terms and among them are:

1) uncertainties regarding the status and scope of aesthetics as a field of study;

2) the problem of disengaging its study from Western assumptions, since so much of its theories appear to be held as dogma; and

3) the methodology of crosscultural studies in aesthetics. (p.4).

We also learn that even scholars like Claude Palisca, Alan Merriam, Marcia Herndon and Norma McLeod take a negative view of aesthetics as a possible area of study in ethnomusicology.

In spite of the uncertainties surrounding this field of enquiry, the literature on ethnomusicology is replete with references to aesthetics and aesthetic issues. For example, studies in African music by scholars like Paul Berliner (1978), J Chernoff (1979) and Charles Keil (1982) demonstrate an interest in the interpretation of African music in both functional and aesthetic terms. Nketia himself reminds us of the particular attention he paid to the aesthetic aspects of musical events in his earlier studies. He informs us in this paper (p.10) that "among the Akan of Ghana, for instance, the two key words used in aesthetic descriptions are *fɛ* (beauty, beautiful) and *dɛ* (sweet, tasty, pleasant). He also provides elaborate observations of Akan musical aesthetics which he claims are applicable to the musical aesthetics of other African societies and may be found to be generally operative in music practised by oral tradition. (pp. 10-12)."

Perhaps the knowledge which is of most worth to the reader in this paper is the identification, by Nketia, of two main lines of enquiry that engage the attention of scholars concerned with aesthetic enquiry and aesthetic theory: "aesthetics as sensuous perception and cognition" and "aesthetics as theory of works of art". (p.14). He adds that they overlap in subject matter and only differ in theoretical emphasis and goals. With regard to the difference between the two, he explains that "aesthetics as theory of works of art" tends to be very specific and limited in its application since it deals with only one type of music, while "aesthetics as sensuous perception and cognition" is general and specific in its application, for it can deal with the totality of a musical culture as well as the specific constraints of individual musical types or the music of different strata and groups in a society. Neither of the two can be ignored in ethnomusicological study of aesthetics. (p.23)

Finally, Nketia draws our attention to the cross-cultural perspectives of aesthetics. He deems it necessary that the socio-cultural factors that operate in the field of aesthetics, including the force of tradition and usage, are correlated with different levels on which the aesthetic dimension is investigated.

The study of aesthetics can be an extension of the ethnomusicologist's investigation into different aspects of music and its socio-cultural context, an extension which, according to Nketia, will take him a step beyond analysis of the use and function of music in culture. Ethnomusicologists need to move from the "ethnographic levels of meaning" or what music means in the lives of various peoples to what it means to those people in aesthetic terms when they hear it. "The importance of such knowledge in our contemporary world of music cannot be overemphasized" concludes Nketia (p.24)

6.2.5 *African Music and Western Praxis: A Review of Western Perspectives on African Musicology*

This paper is a historical review of the contributions of Western scholars, originally from Europe, Britain and America, some of whom settled in Africa, and African scholars, notably from Sierra Leone and Ghana, to the development of African musicology.

Nketia informs us at the beginning of this paper that before the systematic study of African music began in the first decade of the twentieth century, there were numerous references to it in the accounts of early travellers and traders, colonial administrators and missionaries, as well as anthropologists. It should be noted that he had provided brief accounts of the contributions of some of such people, from the West, to the literature on African musical practice and musical instruments in the former Gold Coast (now Ghana) especially in the introductory chapter of his book, *African Music in Ghana* and in his paper, *Ethnomusicology in Ghana*.

We learn from this paper (p.38) that investigations into African music were undertaken by musicologists "who visited different societies for short periods for this purpose, by permanent residents in South Africa such as Percival Kirby and Hugh Tracey; as well as by others like Arthur Jones and Klaus Wachsmann, who took up extended residence in Zambia and Uganda respectively as missionaries, educators, musicologists and museologists". Nketia gives credit to these pioneering scholars for laying the groundwork in African musicology from 1920 to 1950, which he describes as a "period of colonial development". He also mentions other European and British musicologists who continued the study of African music in the field, started by the above-mentioned pioneers, during what he calls "the pre-independence decade" (1950-1960), "the period of Great Transition" (1960-1970) and the following decade. They are: "a new generation" of British scholars such as John Blacking, Anthony King, and David Rycroft; French musicologists such as Hugo Zemp and Simha Arom; and German and Austrian musicologists such as Robert Gunther, Artur Simon, and Gerhard Kubik. Nketia acknowledges the contributions all of them have made to African musicology as well as to the dissemination of information on African music to other Western musicologists and the general public.

We also learn from this paper that it was not only European musicologists who were interested in African musicology. Academic interest in African music, generated by the work of anthropologists of the 1940s, such as Melville Herskovits, and of collectors of African music, such as Laura Boulton had developed from the 1950s onward in the United States of America. The creation of the Society for Ethnomusicology in 1955 also gave a new impetus to the establishment of programmes in ethnomusicology in some American institutions as well as to field work by American scholars and graduate students in different parts of Africa, notably in Uganda, Tanzania, Zambia, Zimbabwe, South Africa, Ghana, Nigeria, Liberia and Gambia.

This paper reveals to us the immense role a scholar and field worker like Hugh Tracey played in the development of folk music and music education in Africa. Nketia (p.39) describes him as someone "who viewed African music first and foremost as an artistic heritage to be shared, preserved, and promoted," and also remarks that "no single individual collected as much over a vast territory as Hugh Tracey". Among Tracey's achievements enumerated by Nketia which may be of interest to us are :

i) He founded the African Music Society in 1947 with Winifred Hoernlé to bring all field workers and interested people together in the hope that their support of African music would lead to the widespread recognition of the integrity of African music and that their collective contributions would lead to "the recognition of distinctive African musicality in Education throughout Africa" *(African Music* 4, no1:5) (see p.46)

ii) He established and edited a newsletter in 1948 which was replaced seven years later by the annual journal *African Music*. This was to ensure that there would be a regular forum for news and articles on African music for members of the Society (p.46). Tracey made strenuous efforts to attract black Africans from the continent to join the society and make contributions to the journal (p.47).

iii) He institutionalised his own research unit and its record-publishing activity which started as the African Music Transcription Library of Gramophone Records and later became the International Library of African Music (ILAM) with John Blacking as its first resident musicologist. (p.46)
It should be noted that ILAM which is sited at Rhodes University in Grahamstown, South Africa, now has a unique collection of African music recordings (the largest in the Southern Hemisphere), instruments and books. (see Ndlovu and Akrofi, 1999:14)

Apart from Hugh Tracey there are other scholars, who through field experience have made significant contributions to African musicology. Some scholars like Lois Anderson, Gerhard Kubik, Andrew Tracey (Hugh's son) and David Locke have continued the work of the pioneer scholars by basing their transcriptions and interpretations of African music on their practical knowledge of the performance techniques of the instruments they deal with. Other scholars like John Chernoff and Paul Berliner attempted to refine theory and the interpretation of African music on the basis of their own experience as students of performance in some African traditions. The technology of instruments, tuning systems, playing techniques, history, and related humanistic issues were explored by Craig Woodson and Cynthia Kimberlin. Nketia also mentions Alan Merriam, Klaus Wachsmann and John Blacking as some of the scholars who have made a significant impact on the theoretical orientations of ethnomusicology.

According to Nketia (p.47-48) there were two landmarks during the colonial period (1920-50): the work of Nicholas George Ballanta of Sierra Leone based on his field work in West Africa sponsored by the Guggenheim Foundation which awarded him two fellowships in 1925 and 1927; and the pioneering work of Ephraim Amu of Ghana in the late 1920s which led to the establishment of courses in African music in Ghana in the 1930s. However, there was no interaction across the continent between these two pioneers in West Africa and the resident musicologists in Uganda, Zambia and South Africa because the colonial period did not make such interaction possible.

The lack of interaction continued from 1950-1960 when Nketia's programme, oriented towards composition, performance and music education, and conceived as a continuation and expansion of the work begun by Amu in the 1920s was established at the University of Ghana. Things looked better in the period 1960-1970 because Africa and the West began to converge, for links with the international world of scholarship were established by African universities and the ministries of Education and Culture through training programmes, participation in international conferences and publications. Nketia (p.49) describes this decade as "the most exciting and challenging period of all for music and musicology in Africa, for the events of the decade established a strong bond between the study of music as an art... and music as a scholarly discipline and focus of research. As a result, the history of music and musicology forms an integral part of the intellectual and cultural history of post-colonial Africa."

We also learn from this paper that during the decade of 1970-1980 more Africans received training in African musicology in Africa and abroad and were able to keep in touch with international scholarship and more especially with the work of Africanists worldwide. This was not possible during the colonial period.

Nketia concludes this paper with two statements which, in my opinion, should be the objectives of current and aspiring scholars of African musicology in Africa and the West:

> What is significant about African scholarship is not what it obviously owes to the West, but what it is able to give back in knowledge and insight as it is shaped by the African environment in which it operates. (p.52)

In our present era, the Western musician and scholar specialising in African musicology has a dual obligation – to Africa and the West. (p.54)

6.2.6 *Contextual Strategies of Inquiry and Systematization*

As mentioned in Chapter four (p.53) of this biographical study, Nketia regards this paper as the "crowning thing" in his career. In his preliminary remarks to this lecture, Nketia, (as quoted in Carter, 1990"xi) says among other things:

> I am particularly happy at what I am doing here at Harvard, not only because I was once here as a Visiting Horatio Appleton Lamb Professor and thoroughly enjoyed it, but also because it was here at Harvard that I gave my first public lecture in the United States in 1958 – exactly 31 years ago, ...Harvard was like a test site and indeed a test case. The response of my audience gave me the confidence to pursue the modes of enquiry and systematization I had begun in Ghana and which it is now my pleasure to elaborate on this occasion... As you can see, returning to Harvard 31 years later to give this lecture is in some sense like coming back to give a valedictory address.

We learn at an early stage of this paper that Nketia (p.79) had a very personal interest in the topic "contextual strategies of inquiry and systematization", for it had been the basis of his own field observations and analytical studies ever since he started his intensive research into African music in 1952 at the University of Ghana. His purpose in this paper was "to present a critique of context and contextualization, using the holism of Seeger as a springboard, while citing here and there some of his corroborative statements and general guidelines". (p.75)

According to Nketia, (p.79), he did not know of Seeger until 1959, but he had long been aware of the heuristic value of context and contextual analysis through his studies in linguistics at the University of London in the 1940s with Professor John R. Firth, who had adapted these concepts in his thinking about speech events and the problem of semantics. Also, Malinowski's use of context as an ethnographic tool appealed to him. Furthermore, the application of the principle of context and contextual analysis as an ethnomusicological technique was discussed briefly in his paper on *The Problem of Meaning in African Music.*

Nketia (p.77) reveals to us that while many people remembered Charles Seeger, in whose memory this lecture is dedicated, for his preoccupation with the term "musicological juncture" he, Nketia, remembered him for the many statements that permeate his writings on what he describes as the "musicological task." He observes that context and contextualization fall within the terms of the musicological task, and quotes the following from Seeger's *Studies in Musicology* (1977:5) to support this view:

> The musicological task cannot be considered much more than begun until by the use of frames of reference, of techniques of comparison, and of other devices of speech presentation, the purely reportorial phase is followed by that of interpretation, and finally by that of integration with the main body of musicological and general thought.

We also learn that although Seeger was one of the four founders of the Society for Ethnomusicology, his reactions to early trends in the discipline of ethnomusicology were critical, for example, his description of ethnomusicology as the "so-called ethnomusicology" or "the bastard offspring" of comparative musicology (1977:15). Seeger also reacted sarcastically to the idea of studying music "in culture" (propagated by scholars like Merriam and supported by Nketia especially in his paper, *(The Problem of Meaning in African Music)*. In his view, the goal of musicology must be "the study of the total music of man both in itself and in its relationship to what is not itself" (1977:108).

Seeger's negative perceptions of some viewpoints in ethnomusicology notwithstanding, Nketia (p.78) points out that he was not against context per se, but was concerned with a particular kind of holism, evident in his suggestions that music phenomena may be "viewed in or out of music contexts" and that this operation constitutes part of "the comprehensive study of systematic musicology" (1977:13).

Nketia believes that Seeger's observations present views that many ethnomusicologists do not dispute even though "we interpret them in our own individual ways". (p.78). He opines :

> It is against this background of Seegerian holism and his idea of "viewing music and musical phenomena in or out of musical contexts" that I would like to discuss contextual strategies of inquiry and systematization.

Nketia gives several reasons for his interest in the contextual approach which, according to him, facilitates the exploration of meaning in music beyond descriptive analysis (p.79). Among them are:

1. People in his own society are more concerned with the meaning or the interpretation of music than with its descriptions. (p.79)

2. The music he had to investigate includes "texts" which exist only in the memory of performers and those who have experienced them, texts that are made manifest in performance. The only way of approaching such musical texts was by observing and documenting them in a variety of

performance contexts as well as contexts in which specific texts could be recalled or discussed by the carriers of the traditions. (p.80)

3. A performance in many ways brings a renewal of shared knowledge and experience and the contextual approach enables one to observe how this experience unfolds both in the musical process and in the interaction of those present. Hence he became committed very early in his field studies to the view of music as a medium for the expression and communication of group sentiments. He cites examples from his previous writings, notably: *Funeral Dirges of the Akan People* (1955) in which he concentrates, among other things, on the exposition of lineage sentiments and how they are communicated, and *Drumming in Akan Communities of Ghana* (1963), several chapters of which are devoted to the relationship between performing groups and performance contexts as well as to descriptions of scenes of drumming in progress intended to convey something of the meaning of drumming to those who take part in particular recreational, social, and ceremonial events. (p.80).

Nketia (p.81) also provides the reader with all the dimensions with regard to the scope of the contextual approach. We are first given a simple definition of "context" as, "any setting or environment – be it physical, ecological, social, cultural or intellectual – in which an entity or a unit of experience is viewed in order to define its identity or characteristics as well as its relations in comparison with other entities or units of experience". The identification of entities in a context therefore involves techniques of observation, while contextualization – the process of viewing such entities in a context in terms of their internal and external relations and relevance – is both analytical and evaluative. Secondly, we learn that contextual frames of reference are open ended as shown in collocations with the word when scholars refer to historical contexts, ethnographic contexts, musical contexts, social contexts, ideological contexts, and so on. Thus every discipline seems to have its favourite contextual frames of reference. Accordingly, there are several frames of reference in which music can be viewed. And thirdly, we are made aware of the fact that there is "consensus among ethnomusicologists that when the word context is used without a qualifier, it means social or cultural context", probably because of the perception that music making is a sociocultural process dominated by human and cultural factors.

With regard to ethnographic context we are told that there is consensus among ethnomusicologists that it is constituted by the occasion and the immediate context of situation sometimes referred to as the context of observation. Nketia (p.83) recommends that we broaden our concept of ethnography in musical research to cover all contexts of music making anywhere in the world in order to end the pride and prejudice set up by our predecessors whose values and commitments in music research were different from ours. He reminds us that there are occasions when music may be promoted as an independent event or as part of other events such as fairs, festivals, religious worship and ritual events or celebrations of the life cycle. Hence it is important to make a distinction between music events, musical events and non music events in contextual studies as he did for example in chapter three of his book *African Music in Ghana* (1962).

We also learn from this paper that descriptions of the ethnographic contexts of music or any other frames of reference are valuable in contextual studies. (p.85). "Contextualization demands more than just describing the social contexts of music" says Nketia, and he quotes Merriam (1964:14) to complement his statement, "for it is also an analytical and evaluative process and should clarify how a people conceptualise their music not only in terms of ideas concerning "music sound" and "music behaviour" but also in respect of their approach to music and music making since patterns of sound and behaviour characteristic of a music culture tend to recur". This in effect means that the approach used by particular societies will determine the nature and scope of the analysis that may be attempted.

Nketia's discussion of the techniques of contextualization includes the following:

> In addition to contextualization of the constituents of the music, the verbal text (the verbal component of the auditory sound events present in songs or implied in instrumental pieces when speech surrogates are used) may similarly be contextualized. (p.86)
>
> Contextualization may be extended to the visual components of a music event – art forms, art object, and kinesic forms that are an integral part of the total performance in order that their reciprocal relations with the auditory components as well as situational and other frames of reference may be identified. (p.86)
>
> It is important to have nexus analysis which involves relationships maintained between music and anything that is integrally or epiphenomenally linked to it. Thus one can examine the nexus between music and institutionalised behaviour, between music and institutional functions, or between music and different domains of human activity, such as religious worship, political and economic activities, and so on. (p.87)

Another interesting technique of contextualization is what Nketia (p.87) calls "factorial analysis", devoted to the external factors perceived to operate in music. "In Seegarian terms," he says "such factors can be described as 'extrinsic pressures brought to bear upon musical processes' and, by extension, the social processes to which they are linked". (p.88). These factors may be causal, physical, social, political, economic, cultural, or historical. Thus one may distinguish between the nexus relationship between music and social, political or economic activities on the one hand, and on the other, the pressures exerted on music and music making by social, political or economic forces which may result in varying forms of control of music or the use of music as an agent of social and political control, or protest. Nketia advises the ethnomusicologist not to focus only on the effect of all these factors on music making but also to look at the reverse since influences are reciprocal. He says:

> For example, in a study of music and society, the scholar may observe not only the effect of social factors on music, but also the impact of music on society, individual behaviour, consciousness of identity, and so forth. (p.88)

Looking at contexualization from another angle, Nketia observes that for the ethnomusicologist who has expertise in a cognate discipline, contextualization might enable him/her to contribute to particular topics in that discipline or to the development of its theory from an ethnomusicological perspective. He cites Seeger's (1977:5) suggestion that, integrating ethnomusicological findings into the main body of musicological and general thought should follow the "reportorial, analytical and evaluative phases of our work".

Nketia concludes this paper with a discussion of how ethnomusicological theories of music are conceived. He writes:

> If contextualization is a process which enables the scholar to clarify approaches to music and music making and the relationships and meanings that are established, it should lead in the final analysis to the systematization of formal and contextual data and the formulation of ethnomusicological theories of music. In this connection we must note that data on musical events and technical information derived from the analysis of such events provide knowledge on the most basic level. They do not become theoretical knowledge in ethnomusicological terms until they are systematized or processed on a higher level of abstraction.

Taking into account the reciprocal relationships between music and its contexts and the Seegerian ideal of integrating formal and contextual data which he upholds, Nketia (p.92) formulates three ethnomusicological theories of music relevant to the musical experience: the formal, the social, and the semantic.

Formal theories deal with sounds and systems of

sounds, structures, textures and densities, compositional processes and procedures, and elements of performance practice. This area of theory according to him is critical for understanding the communicative potential of music as a creative and aesthetic experience.

Social theories in his view deal with the role and function of music and music making in the context of social relations. There is a tendency to link music, music makers, and the social perceptions of musical performance. This area of theory is,therefore, critical for understanding the communicative potential of music as a social experience.

Semantic theories of music deal with the semantic implications of the formal and the social theories discussed above. Nketia regards this area of theory as critical for understanding the communicative potential of music as a cultural experience. He asserts that the importance of these three theories of music cannot be overemphasized.

It is appropriate for Nketia to end this lecture/paper dedicated to the memory of Charles Seeger with comments relating to some of the corroborative statements of the latter:

> To ensure that such theories are based on empirical data and not on speculation, it is always important, as Seeger once remarked, to "refer verbal theory back to music practice", first because as he notes "a principal aim of scholarly

> work is to effect the closest possible correspondence between the results of study and what is studied "(Seeger 1968:33). And second because if we do this, "we may not only benefit from practice but keep theory from running off the rails "(Seeger 1968:38). It is because of this that I have dwelt at length on contextual techniques of analysis and systematization which, in my experience, enable the scholar to keep the primary focus and concerns of his discipline constantly in mind, for whatever conceptual framework of reference we choose, our analysis and interpretation must enrich our understanding of music and its relationship to its contexts. (p.93)

This paper, is indeed, a piece of scholarly work which musicologists, ethnomusicologists and students pursuing advanced studies in ethnomusicology ought to include in their reading lists.

6.2.7 *Music and Cultural Policy in Contemporary Africa*

This paper is a review of attempts made by post-independent countries in Africa to produce official documents on their national cultural policies. Nketia begins it with a definition of cultural policy, taken from an unidentified UNESCO publication on national cultural policies:

... a set of operational principles which guide the planning of cultural programmes, the establishment of institutions, and the making of administrative and budgetary provisions for the implementation of these.

We learn from the paper that the institutions mentioned in the above definition include "educational institutions, arts councils and similar agencies; libraries, archives and museums; concert halls and symphony orchestras; theatre, opera and ballet companies; art galleries; publishing houses, radio, television, and the film industry, all of which are typical organs of cultural life in industrialized countries." (p.77). We are also informed that the documents on cultural policy in African countries also list the aforementioned institutions as organs of culture in contemporary Africa. New institutions in the colonial or post-colonial periods, such as language bureaus, national dance companies or cultural troupes which supplement or replace symphony orchestras and other western-type performing groups are also mentioned in connection with cultural development.

In view of the existence of both Western and contemporary cultural institutions in Africa, Nketia advises that African nations encourage "the building of bridges between ethnic cultures as well as the integration of the old and the new, indigenous and foreign, and the modalities of cultural exchange." (p.78). Thus cultural policy in Africa should be transformative and to a large extent developmental.

As Nketia observes, colonialism and Western culture pushed African cultural expressions and values from the forefront to the background, and led to cultural alienation. He discusses in this paper attempts made by some progressive artists and educators of the colonial period to combat this trend.

We saw in Nketia's paper, *African Music and Western Praxis: A Review of Western Perspectives on African Musicology* the contributions of two pioneer African scholars, George Ballanta of Sierra Leone and Ephraim Amu of Ghana, to the development of African cultural traditions in music. Aside from these two pioneers, another African is introduced to us in this paper, and he is "Ruben Tolakele Caluza of South Africa who felt that African music should be taken seriously not only in the Christian church, but also in the general world of entertainment and formal education". (p.80) We learn that Caluza collected Zulu songs and recorded some of these and his own compositions in London with his choir in 1930 and also advocated the collection and preservation of African songs.

The search for African cultural identity and values pursued by African educators and scholars, including the above named musicians/musicologists, resulted in the need for social and national integration through the arts, especially after independence. Nketia (p.82) identifies two fields of social and cultural action developed as a result of colonial intervention : the traditional and the contemporary. He explains that in the traditional setting behaviour is guided by factors of ethnicity, kinship, and a common indigenous language and culture. Emphasis is laid on ceremonies, rituals and festivals for expressing and consolidating the bonds that bind social groups. Music and dance in this setting are performed as recreational activities or as part of a larger event and, therefore, do not require separate institutions for their promotion. The contemporary setting on the other hand comprises linkages established through membership in establishments such as educational institutions, churches and religious associations, trade unions, political parties, sports clubs and organizations, market unions, factories and so on. Unlike the traditional setting, musical activities in the contemporary setting tend to be organized by individuals, organizations, institutions, promoters of the arts, cultural officers, or organizers of political events.

The two fields of social and cultural action according to Nketia have influenced the structure of musical and cultural programmes upon which cultural policies are determined. Furthermore tradition and innovation are part of national cultural policies and institutional support for the training of contemporary musicians and dancers in both traditional and non-traditional music and dance now forms part of the cultural policies of African governments.

Nketia's discussion of the implications of cultural policy for scholarly research reminds us of his field research in the 1940s and 1950s which resulted in the birth of ethnomusicology in Ghana. He recommends that contemporary Africa should have scholars with a humanistic orientation – African scholars conversant with the problems and needs of their own intellectual, social and cultural environment, and Western ethnomusicologists sympathetic to contemporary African aspirations who will go to Africa to work in partnership with their African colleagues or policy makers. African scholars are also advised to co-operate with their counterparts not only in the West but also within Africa. Nketia (p.91) says: "…there is no reason why African ministries and departments of culture cannot invite the collaboration of African musicologists or make use of training programmes in other African countries".

Finally, Nketia talks about the need for new research paradigms which will take into account "contemporary social structures and social life and the influence of the ideologies of African cultural policies on tradition, creativity and innovation" (p.92). Scholars are, therefore, advised to approach their research both from a scholarly perspective as historians of musical cultures and the perspective of music makers who are constantly involved in the creative interpretation of tradition and change.

6.2.8 *National Development and the Performing Arts of Africa*

We learn from the onset of this paper that modern African states attach importance to the performing arts which are valued not only for their traditional role as a source of aesthetic enjoyment and a medium of communication but also for their creative potential and the contemporary role they play in national development. Nketia argues, and justifiably so, that national development is applicable not only to technology and material things of life but also to any aspect of a people's way of life such as is portrayed in the performing arts.

We glean from this paper that the performing arts are music, dance, theatre, folklore and oral literature. Nketia classifies the performing arts into two categories of traditional and contemporary which he clearly defined and described in his paper, *"Music and Cultural Policy in Contemporary Africa"* (discussed in 6.2.7 above). It should be noted that both the traditional arts and contemporary arts complement each other.

To people who fear that the rapid social changes taking place in Africa today will lead to a situation in which the traditional arts will die or disappear, Nketia assures them that the privilege he had of doing fieldwork enables him to testify that "the traditional arts are 'living' arts and not 'relics' of the past or 'folk arts' that survive only in the memory of a few" (p.2). Among the examples he cites to support his optimistic view are Hugh Tracey's devotion to the recording and documentation of traditional African music, the resilience of traditional performing arts in the Caribbean and the Americas and the cultivation of traditional arts in many rural and urban communities in many regions of Africa. As he did in his earlier writings, notably, *African Music in Ghana, Drumming in Akan Communities of Ghana,* and *The Music of Africa,* Nketia reiterates in this paper the importance of instrumental resources – musical instruments used independently as well as accompaniment to singing and dancing, and for a variety of other functions (see Nketia, 1974:69-115)

Nketia's discussion of contemporary arts in the context of nation building, Pan African and global perspectives reveal the following:

> Traditional arts constitute the most visible and dynamic testimony of the achievements of the African past. They assume a dual status on the attainment of independence from colonial rule as community arts cultivated and practised on the basis of ethnicity and as national arts which could be performed on national occasions as well as other contemporary contexts. (p.11)
>
> The arts contribute to nation building, in particular the process of creating and maintaining new institutional frameworks and loyalties that transcend the boundaries of ethnicity. Accordingly National Arts Festivals were instituted in African countries after independence for promoting unity in diversity by getting performers and audiences from different regions to interact and share cultural experiences (p.12).

The philosophy of Négritude advocated by the late first President of Senegal, Leopold Senghor, resulted in the first World Festival of Negro Arts held in Dakar in 1966. This was followed by: (i) the Algiers Festival of Arts held in 1972 under the auspices of the Organisation of African Unity (OAU) which emphasized the political dimension of the arts by including Arab North Africa excluded from the first festival; (ii) FESTAC (Festival of Arts and Culture) held in Lagos, Nigeria, January 15 to February 12, 1977 in collaboration with all the governments in Africa, and which extended the coverage of the two previous festivals to Africans in the Diaspora and thus promoted the worldwide concept of Black culture.

The enormous problems involved in organising inter-African arts festivals of such magnitude and economic decline faced by many African countries have held such programmes in abeyance (p.13).

Nketia concludes this paper with the suggestion that performing arts institutions in Africa are strengthened so that they can also build bridges between tradition and change in their course offerings and practical training programmes as well as act as spearheads in culture and development in their areas of specialization. (p.25) Where a country does not have performing arts institutions, he proposes the creation of research units which can initiate and implement programmes in conjunction with relevant departments and cultural organizations. He mentions the establishment of the Institute of African Studies and the School of Music, Dance and Drama at the University of Ghana in the 1960s as worthy ventures which enabled him not only to do extensive research but also to participate actively in the development of cultural programmes.

The following is a befitting 'coda' to this paper:

> While the development intervention assumed by Governments soon after independence was inevitable, the time has come to adopt other approaches that will enable imaginative individuals, various arts associations and institutions as well as Non-Governmental Organisations to contribute in their own way to growth and development of performing arts of Africa. The International Center for African Music and Dance and Regional Organizations in cognate fields can play a co-ordinating role in such initiatives. (p.27)

6.2.9 The Challenge of Cultural Preservation in a Dynamic Social Environment

Since this paper was written for delivery at a National Festival of Arts in Ghana, the issues raised in it are applicable to the social environment in Ghana.

Nketia first expresses concern that cultural preservation, inherent in the philosophy of African personality or the principle of *sankofa* (the retrieval or revival of culture), pursued ardently in Ghana in the exciting post-independence periods has not been able to maintain its momentum and its impact on creativity. (p.2). He blames tokenism and cosmetic changes in the creative field and also Ghana's approach to institution building for this state of affairs. Our attention is drawn to the fact that tokenism runs through many facets of Ghanaian society, including the educational system where, until the 1980s, a course in cultural studies or some African topic was added as a cosmetic change. Other acts of tokenism still prevalent in Ghana today are: "choral groups whose preference is for Handel's *Messiah* and similar great works and English anthems include one or two Ghanaian compositions in their repertoire as a token of their response to the quest for something indigenous"; and Christian churches which "now use gospel and new compositions in the style of Highlife as diversions". (p.7)

"The challenge we face today", says Nketia, "is not only that of recognizing the validity of our traditional cultures for the purpose of generating appropriate levels of consciousness as was done during the period of cultural nationalism but also that of redefinition of the place our own cultures should occupy in our social, political and religious life as well as in our contemporary institutions, and the manner in which the creative use or possible application of the accumulated wisdom and forms of knowledge of our forebears and surviving custodians of traditional arts and culture can be promoted in contemporary contexts". (p.2-3)

Perhaps the best way of confronting the challenge he observes is to approach the task of cultural preservation on all fronts, using both the oral methods as was the case in the past and the technical means now available to us for the preservation of culture. This can be achieved through the establishment of cultural archives in Ghana and Nketia (p.5) advises that every effort should be made to disseminate materials from such archives in a form that can be of value to artists – composers, choreographers, dramatists, performers and educators.

According to Nketia (p.6) the emergence of contemporary contexts of social and cultural life have emerged which raise other challenges. Among his suggestions for strengthening existing cultural processes and thereby creating a society that lives in a dynamic environment are:

> The preservation through appropriate promotion programmes, research and audio visual documentation of the traditional sources of creativity maintained in ethnic communities.
>
> The involvement of leading exponents of traditional culture, creative performers, and outstanding ensembles in contemporary cultural programmes.

The acceleration of transfer of knowledge, skills and repertoire from traditional environments into contemporary settings through educational programmes and the media.

He feels that these can be achieved through co-operation among cultural experts, artists, critics as well as institutional, corporate and public support for the arts. He also proposes the formation of arts associations and networks that bring people together to review aspects of Ghanaian art and culture so that there will always be shared consensus coming from the people themselves which can guide national cultural policy.

6.2.10 *Intellectual Agenda for Coping with Social Reality*

This is the only one out of the ten papers reviewed in this chapter which does not deal specifically with a topic concerning music or the arts. In his capacity as President of the Ghana Academy of Arts and Sciences, Nketia addresses the cream of Ghana's intelligentsia. The reason he gives for the selection of this topic is "because this concept has always been part of the rationale for the creation of an Academy of Arts and Sciences as a national institution for the recognition of excellence in intellectual achievement in Ghana" (p.1). He also informs us that "the Academy has always been interested in providing a platform for the exchange of views and ideas about our social reality and the strategies for coping with the problems and issues that emerge from time to time". (p.2)

Some of the ideas in this paper are taken from sources by philosophers. In the first instance, the definition of the concept of an intellectual is taken from the standpoints of two outstanding Ghanaian philosophers; Kwame Gyekye and Kwame Appiah, both of whom list intellectuals as academics, clergymen, diplomats, civil servants, educators and writers. Secondly, we are taken through the observations of the British philosopher and mathematician, Alfred Whitehead. Nketia describes his book, *Adventures of Ideas*, published in 1933, as "remarkable" and recommends it to his Ghanaian audience because the ideas in it "are pertinent to the formulation of intellectual agendas". (p.3)

Nketia also provides us with two basic assumptions central to Whitehead's discussion. The first is that what defines the state of the culture and civilization of a people or development in any given period is the font of ideas generated by creative thinkers or the intellectuals of a nation, and the second is that ideas have a life of their own as well as their qualitative aspects. From these two assumptions, Nketia arrives at the following he considers relevant to the situation in Ghana:

> The presence of practical men and women who combine understanding with know-how, and intellectuals who give themselves time to reflect on their world of reality is essential, for there is

a humanistic dimension of development that must go hand in hand with economic and technological development (p.3)

...no matter where they come from, a critical assessment of ideas is necessary, first because they embody the boundaries of mental experiences of individual thinkers in particular historical and cultural environments, and second, because they influence attitudes and modes of action. (p.4)

Furthermore, we are furnished with three Whiteheadian broad areas in which mental experiences function as formative elements of culture:

1. the sociological – in his terms, everything to do with human life

2. the cosmological – ideas related to nature as observed or experienced reality and its influence on world view and behaviour, and

3. the philosophical – ideas related to the nature of things, knowledge, notions, concepts, principles, process and relations, including the relationships between the methods and theories of science and the abstract generalizations of philosophical inquiry. (p.4)

Nketia (p.5) reveals to us that his interest in Whitehead's philosophy led him during the 1940s, when he was a student in London, out of curiosity, to go outside his own fields of specialization to read the works of other philosophers like Bertrand Russell, Ayer and Carnap which kindled his interdisciplinary inclinations. Indeed, in this paper, his quotation from Whitehead, "a civilized society is one that exhibits or pursues the five qualities of Truth, Beauty, Adventure, Art and Peace" is used as a basis for facing challenges of the social reality of Ghana today.

"Our contemporary social reality", says Nketia, "is marked by a duality of old and new, indigenous and foreign, the products of science and technology as well as those of traditional arts and crafts, the art forms of traditional and contemporary Africa as well as those of other lands, ..." (p.8) He adds that the reason for this duality is too well known to us. "It is a reality that will continue to develop, first because we live in a world dominated by Western structures and ideas that are continually being globalized, and second, because we do not have all the structures and infrastructures we need for maintaining or carrying the exogenous component of our way of life forward or for responding to the pressures and challenges of global economy, global politics, and so on" (p.9)

The intellectual challenge, we are told, is how we make sense of the duality or use the legacy of colonial development and post-colonial adoptions as a springboard for change and development inspired by our own mental activities and mental experience.

What is the nature of the intellectual agenda for coping with social reality? According to Nketia, (p.10-11) such an intellectual agenda must address itself to three areas:

1. It must address the issue of mentality or established modes of thinking that contribute to or hinder the creation of a harmonious social environment for development. This category includes traditional mentality, colonial mentality, dependency syndrome and paternalism.

2. The second area concerns creating and promoting an environment receptive to ideas related to the pursuit of Truth, Beauty, Art, Adventure and Peace, an environment for nurturing the capacity for intellectual reflection and creativity since it is these that trigger innovation, however modest, in human societies.

3. The third area aims at building individual capacity for knowledge and understanding and the ability to make critical judgements essential for the promotion of development

On the role of the Academy, Nketia (p.14) observes that meaningful development is impossible without some sort of vision that allows for systematic planning and periodic review. It is in light of this that the Academy has devoted part of its agenda to the review of problems and prospects in science and technology, health and health delivery systems, and the problem of the "uneasy" alliance of traditional and modern medicine and practices in Ghana, and has occasionally provided a platform for Ghanaian scientists, especially those joining the Academy as Fellows, to tell us about their research findings.

Finally, we learn that documents like the Proceedings of the Academy of Arts and Sciences and other publications are "a rich mine of information and suggestions for dealing with some of our problems". (p.16). Nketia remarks that the time has come for the Academy to make such information available in a different and more digestible and readily accessible format such as an Academy Digest that would be published quarterly or half yearly, to which readers would subscribe and which could present suitable excerpts and short articles that individuals in all parts of Ghana could read and digest.

With the exception of *Folk Songs of Ghana* and *The Music of Africa*, Nketia's other four books on African musicology discussed in this chapter, are out-of-print and thus difficult to obtain. *Akanfoɔ Nnwom Bi*, for example is the most inaccessible of the six books. Nketia's wish that this book would inspire present generation of Ghanaians to learn some of the songs it contains which are becoming extinct may therefore, not come true for the following reasons:

1. Although the majority of Ghanaians are Akan, very few educated Ghanaians can read or write Twi. The fact that this book is written in Twi means that it will attract an insignificant readership.

2. As mentioned earlier, there are no English translations of the Twi texts nor music examples in this book as is the case in the other books. Readers, therefore, have no idea what each of the 164 songs (texts only) sounds like.

Since magnetic tape recorders were non existent in Ghana in the early 1940s we cannot presume that recordings of all the songs, the texts of which appear in *Akanfoɔ Nnwom Bi* are available. As the Institute of African Studies and the International Centre for African Music and Dance now have large holdings of traditional Ghanaian songs in their Archives, Nketia's pioneer work can be followed up. A revised and enlarged edition of the book incorporating other categories of songs not included in the original and accompanying CD and English translations of the texts will enable the present generation to have a more meaningful experience of not only the words but also the musical sounds of the songs.

Of the ten papers on ethnomusicology cum African music and culture, five of them deal with his views on philosophical issues notably meaning, aesthetics and contextualization. Although Nketia constantly refers to his fieldwork research in Ghana, his discussions, in these five papers, are not based primarily on indigenous African theories but rather show the influence of the ideas of Western scholars like Firth, Merriam, Seeger and Whitehead. Could the ideas of African scholars or philosophers not have been handy in the papers in question or were there no such persons whose thoughts were relevant in the field of African musicology?

Viewed in terms of the time frame in which the five theoretical papers were written, and the readership for which they were intended, it is evident that Nketia's primary concern was not with trends in African musicology (which was steadily gaining recognition) or African philosophy but with the clarification and presentation of alternative modes of enquiry and interpretation suggested by African materials and insights from field work or the challenge of African realities. Since his African colleagues had then not approached the particular issues he dealt with from the same perspective, his strategy was to use ideas of the scholars he cites who are recognised experts in their fields as points of departure.

CHAPTER SEVEN

NKETIA'S THOUGHTS ON MUSIC EDUCATION

Kwabena Nketia's thoughts on music education are expressed in a dozen papers he wrote between the 1960s and 1980s and delivered mostly at international conferences and seminars. Seven of the papers are discussed in this chapter.

7.1.1 *Music Education in African Schools*

His first paper on music education, "Music Education in African Schools : A Review of the Position in Ghana", was read at an International Seminar on Teacher Education in Music held at the University of Michigan, Ann Arbor, U.S. in 1966. It is one of the most significant early contributions to the literature on Ghanaian public school music education (Akrofi, 1982:12). In this paper, Nketia described the organisation of institutional methods of music instruction used in classrooms in Ghana and sub-Saharan Africa in the 1960s He asserted that these methods posed problems for the music teacher in Ghana and explained that:

> As music is traditionally practiced in African communities as an integral part of social life, there is the danger that musical activities in the classroom – an artificially created musical situation – may be unrelated to experience in

society. There is the danger that the teacher might treat music merely as an object of instruction rather than as something vital, alive and part of experience (Nketia, 1966:231).

Nketia suggested that it was the responsibility of the teacher to make music live under classroom conditions. It was also the duty of the music teacher to organise systematic instruction in all fields of music to enhance and not hinder the cultivation of love for music characteristic of the African way of life. He conceded that there were many problems to be tackled if the music teacher in African schools were to fulfil such expectations. In his opinion, the most pressing of these problems are :

>...those arising out of the cross-cultural situation in which Africa now finds itself, and which tends to give undue prestige or importance to elements of foreign cultures at the expense of corresponding indigenous forms. This is particularly noticeable in music education, for before the advent of Western education in Africa (introduced largely by missionaries, traders, and colonial governments), the classroom situation did not exist. (ibid., p.232)

Nketia feels that this cross-cultural situation has resulted in a deliberate isolation of educated Africans and Christian converts from the music and cultures of their own people. He adds that nationalism and a growing awareness of African cultural values in post-independent African nations have caused contemporary African educators to question and alter the cross-cultural situation in which the music teacher in Africa finds himself. He cites the publication of the *Music Syllabus for Primary Schools* in 1959, by the Ministry of Education in Ghana as one of the first steps taken in this direction. According to him, this syllabus sought to bridge the musical gap between the educated Ghanaian and his cultural environment, between music in schools and music in community life, and to make the music of Africa the starting point of music education. The Syllabus also represented an attempt to bring African music into the activities of the classroom alongside Western music. Commenting on this syllabus, Nketia said it was not satisfactory in all respects because its conception of music education and curriculum organisation were based on European or British models, with the result that the realities of the African situation were not fully met. He stated that:

> The provision of a syllabus thus offers only a partial solution to the problem of organizing musical activities in the classroom. To be worthwhile, it must be preceded by a search for a clear definition of aims and objectives so that music education in post-colonial Africa does not continue as a mere extension of missionary or colonial educational aims but something based on how contemporary Africans see music

education in relation to their society, remembering that music education can be at once an instrument of change and a means of fostering and preserving the music values of a culture (ibid. p.239)

Following this statement, he makes the following suggestions he deems relevant in the preparation of an ideal music syllabus for Ghana or any African country:

1. The music of Africa – the music of the child's home and environment – should be made the starting point of music education especially in primary school,
2. Music syllabuses must be backed by the right kind of training of those whose duty it is to teach music in schools. Music education in teacher training colleges must be given the proper attention it deserves,
3. The music syllabus must be backed by the provision of the proper kind of material, for example, African folk songs used must be available in a carefully graded form,
4. The music syllabus must be based on sound African pedagogic principles which should provide the basis for syllabuses or for working out detailed teaching programs based on such syllabuses.

Perhaps the most problematic of the above suggestions for African music educators especially in the 1960s, is the last. Nketia (ibid. p.240) lists the African pedagogic principles as follows:

a. Awareness of the African approach to music, and, in particular, the musical procedures that are applied in African music.
b. An understanding of the structure of African music and the learning processes that it requires.
c. A knowledge of the psychology of African music, in particular a knowledge of the musical background of the pre-school child in different African environments, rural and urban, the level and extent of his capacity for discrimination in pitch, rhythm, etc.

He however, concedes that in many of these areas, the music teacher in Africa is handicapped because: (1) he has no indigenous tradition of music pedagogy of a systematic nature to guide him; he is himself a product of acculturation and his training may show a bias of a type which may now be his task to eradicate from the educational system; (2) the material he needs is not always available. For example, if he has to teach African folk songs, he must search for his own material and learn to sing the songs himself. Furthermore, if he has to teach African instruments which he has never learned to play himself, he must face the task of learning to do so; (3) he has not cultivated a broad outlook in music or widened his horizon to include the music of other African cultures.

Nketia concludes this paper with a suggestion that Ghana and other African countries review and overhaul the music education programmes in their schools. He feels that the gap between music in the classroom and music in the community can be bridged if the study of music education is combined with the study of ethnomusicology in music teacher education programmes in Ghana and sub-Saharan Africa.

7.1.2   *The Place of Authentic Folk Music in Education*

Nketia's paper, "The Place of Authentic Folk Music in Education" was presented as a speech at the International Society for Music Education Biennial Conference held at Interlochen, Michigan, U.S. on August 24, 1966. It was published in the *Music Educators Journal* 54(3) in November 1967. Some of his views on music education expressed in his paper discussed above are echoed in this paper. However, his premise in the latter is that music education should provide a link between the school and the community. He said:

> It should aim at providing education as well as a link between the school and the community, between music in school and the musical life outside it. Therefore, no program of music education that sets out to be

> comprehensive can ignore various areas of musical activity that are entrenched in the life of a society and are recognized as culturally valid. That is why it would, for example, be wrong for Africa to ignore its traditional music, as was done in the colonial period, or to give exclusive attention to Western music which is peripheral to the culture of Africa (Nketia, 1967:41).

He argues that what he has said for Africa can be applied to many other countries that treasure their folk music and use it as a basis for the musical education of their children. He mentions Hungary as a notable example of countries that have made headway in certain directions, such as the exploitation of folk music material for a variety of instructional purposes but laments that many countries do not "make progress beyond satisfying the tourist trade, recognizing folk music as fashionable social music, or organizing highly entertaining folk music festivals". (p.41)

Nketia draws the attention of music educators to the attributes that make folk music worthy of inclusion in the school music curriculum. He states:

> The folk music of a country may represent not only a heritage of individual items of music but also music that speaks its own kind of language, music that has a distinctive vocabulary of its own, evident in its choice of scales, use of modes; characteristic emphasis on particular intervals, cadential patterns, melodic

contours, meters, and rhythmic combination, as well as its vocal techniques and singing style. Therefore, folk music should be recognized as a distinct musical idiom, with its own traditions, musical instruments, performance technique, and its own set of values that may not necessarily be the same as those associated with art music. Only when the music educator realizes this and is willing to consider folk music in its own terms can he use it systematically in his programme. (p.41)

With regard to the use of folk music in education on the continent of Africa, Nketia expects that such music would include songs, instrumental music, combined instrumental and vocal forms, movement which goes with instrumental techniques and movement demanded of singers in different situations; as well as dances; the oral literature which forms an essential component of folk music and the traditions that govern the practice of this music, including its contextual organization. He argues that folk music cannot properly be studied in isolation and therefore, proposes an interdisciplinary study of it which will require the music teacher to "correlate music and movement, music and language, music and arts and crafts, and music and drama" (p.129). This, according to him, will enable the music teacher to translate musical learning into a meaningful social activity. Nketia cites story telling as an example which combines many of the disciplines mentioned above:

> It involves a narrator and a chorus, the singing of song interludes, drumming, dancing, and miming. Everyone becomes involved in one way or another at a story-telling session, and this should be exploited in the classroom. (p.129)

Another important suggestion Nketia makes in this paper is concerned with the study of musical instruments and their uses in the performance of folk music. He observes that Africa is rich in percussion and proposes that a start can be made in the school music programme with such instruments, particularly in rhythm training which is a very important area of study in African music.

Nketia concludes this paper by stating emphatically that the African approach makes folk music the basis as well as the material of music education. He says:

> Ultimately, whether in Hungary or Ghana, the music educator must approach his task with an intimate knowledge of his folk music material. (p.133)

7.1.3 *Music Education in African and the World*

In his capacity as Vice-President of ISME, Kwabena Nketia presented a paper, "Music Education in Africa and the West: We can Learn from Each Other" to the first General Session of the ISME Congress in Moscow, U.S.S.R. on July 9, 1970. The article was published in the *Music Educators Journal 57(3)* in November 1970. He begins this paper with a discussion of the musical development of the child as an individual and potential maker, user, or consumer of music especially in Western societies. He feels this is laudable:

> There is no doubt, of course, that concentration on the child as an individual is of vital importance in music and indeed the other arts, and should remain a primary objective (p.48)

However, he reminds music educators of the existence of a social dimension to music education which necessitates that music be studied in terms of the context of society and the context of culture. He states:

> Our task as educators, therefore, is not only to impart knowledge and skills or nurture creativity in children, but also to contribute to the development of the personality of the child who lives his life both as an individual and as a member of social groups (p.48).

He feels the socio-musical development of the child should be the concern of music educators as it would ensure that every child developed not only musical responsiveness, understanding, and aesthetic sensitivity, but also a critical awareness of how music is practised in his society.

According to Nketia, the community-oriented musical education he recommends to his Western audience is well suited to traditional Africa. However, he continues:

> It is clear from the changes that have already taken place as a result of the impact of Western culture and technology on Africa that musical life that depends solely on informal processes of enculturation for its survival cannot endure the pressures of the modern world. In a community-oriented music education program for contemporary Africa, therefore, it is necessary that the learning process be systematized and organized on some formal basis (p.54).

Nketia concludes this paper with a discussion of the strengths and weaknesses of the two approaches of music education he examined in relation to the life of the community or in relation to the development of the individual. He observes that many Western countries with their highly developed institution-oriented music education programmes do not appear to be sufficiently community-oriented whereas Africa with its strong community-oriented approach is weak in its institutional approach to the development of the individual. He sees a solution to these problems in the establishment of:

> ...a unified approach to music education in all societies, involving very close collaboration between two groups of educators: those responsible for the education of the youth in schools, and those responsible for the arts

education of the general public and the community (p.55)

7.1.4 *Music Education in Contemporary Africa*

And finally, he advises that music educators in Africa and the West be fully aware of the nexus between all levels of music education and the musical life of the community.

In his paper, "The Objectives of Music Education in Contemporary Africa", read at the Lusaka Music Conference, Zambia, held in June 15-22, 1971, Kwabena Nketia again expressed concern (as he did in his two 1966 papers discussed earlier in this chapter) about the influence of the colonial music education system on the music education programme in contemporary Africa when he wrote:

> I do not believe that the kind of reform that we need is merely one that substitutes African materials for items in the syllabuses based on the colonial music education system, for these reflect a structure of music education which was not really conceived from within, from the point of view of African musical values or the role of music in our social life. The structure is geared to Western musical institutions -- to the concert hall, the theatre, as well as Western concepts of performance-audience relationships, Western theory of music, Western aesthetics and so forth (p.7).

He warns Africans, not to follow the Western system of music education blindly without considering the nexus between music and their society or what their objectives should be with regard to the needs of Africa.

7.1.5 *Research and Education in African Music*

Writing in his capacity as editor of articles written by music educators in Ghana in a publication titled *Notes on Education and Research in African Music* by the Institute of African Studies, University of Ghana, Legon in 1975, Nketia shows his disappointment with the content and methods of music teaching and learning in Ghana as follows:

> Anyone who observes music lessons in our schools or examines the syllabuses in current use cannot fail to notice the somewhat lowly position that African music still occupies. Not only does one find little originality in the approach to the teaching of the subject, but also much of what is presented does not appear to offer the kind of challenge that would stimulate further exploration of the techniques and materials of this music outside the classroom, or encourage meaningful participation in traditional music as a form of community experience. It is important, therefore, that we remind ourselves from time to time of our objectives and review our approach to music teaching generally and the quality and content of our courses. (p.5)

7.1.6 New Perspectives in Music Education

Kwabena Nketia delivered another significant speech on the topic "New Perspectives in Music Education" at an ISME International Seminar in Lisbon, Portugal in 1978 and it was published in the *ISME Yearbook V* of the same year. The concern of this paper, according to Nketia, is "the institutional aspect of music education"(p.111). He began his delivery with the statement:

> Throughout the ages, the primary objective of education has been the transmission of a society's cultural heritage – its heritage of ideas, beliefs, modes of thought, values, forms of knowledge and skills as well as its works of art in the plastic, visual and sound medium. Custodians of musical knowledge in traditional societies have tended to emphasise this objective, while their modern counterparts with a much more refined philosophy of education which seeks the development of the potential of the individual nevertheless show a concern for a realistic relation to their heritage of music in their teaching programmes (p.104)

Thereafter, he discussed the limitations in perspective of the above stated objective of music education. Of particular concern to Nketia is the little attention given to folk and popular music especially in Western music programmes. He says:

> …in some countries the folk song belongs to

> the Department of Folklore and not to the Department or School of Music, just as some western institutions tolerate the study of the music of Africa and Asia in Departments of Anthropology and Linguistics but not in their Departments of Music. (p.105)

He continues:

> ...it has taken long for jazz to be considered as something worthy of systematic instruction in High Schools and Tertiary Institutions. Even in the United States, courses in jazz and Afro-American music for that matter are offered in some University Institutions with Black Studies programmes and not as it should be in the regular Departments of Music. (p.105)

These statements show that the programme of systematic instruction of the cultural heritage approach to music education does not always reflect all the musical expressions that form the basis of the musical life of a country. Nketia therefore, calls for the development of new attitudes in the cultural heritage approach to music education. His tripartite model, which identifies music as a vehicle of cultural education, music as a tool of education to exploit its potential as a communication medium, and music education as a basis of cultural transformation rejects the third approach which he describes as "one-sided, resulting in cultural alienation". (p.108). He asserts that music education in the twentieth century should avoid: "the use of music education as a tool of cultural transformation resulting in cultural alienation rather than in cultural enrichment". (ibid). He proposes what he calls "a philosophy of bi-musicality" as an educational concept which "offers a happier compromise and prospect for better intercultural relations in the future". But, perhaps a better future for music education lies in the creation of a new world order which Nketia suggests will enable the musician and the music lover "to grow at once as citizens of their respective countries and citizens of interacting world communities" (p.109).

Nketia feels the intercultural music education programme he recommends in this paper should lay considerable emphasis on aesthetics as a basis of approach to " all aspects of music, including the perception, analysis, evaluation and interpretation of sound materials, form, structure, modes of expression and presentation as well as contextual organisation" (p.110).

He concludes this paper with a recommendation that concerted international effort be made to intensify and expand intercultural music education of the youth in all regions of the world through their normal school curriculum and extra curricular activities. He suggests the following which will result in the achievement of this objective:

1. That UNESCO be asked to set up centres similar to those set up in Iran and Japan for the compilation of children's

songs and other cultural materials that can be used regionally and elsewhere in intercultural studies;

2. That ISME be encouraged to set up Commissions for intercultural music studies in co-operation with the Regional Secretariats of the IMC for the purpose of stimulating the preparation of curricular materials based on the resources of each region on sound pedagogical lines;

3. That in co-operation with IMC and ISME, the International Institute for Comparative Music Studies and Documentation be asked to explore all avenues for convening a series of small meetings of experts to work out pilot programmes for the selection, grading, preparation and exchange of documentary and audio-visual materials, drawing largely on materials accumulated through the work of the different Music Rostrums organised by IMC and the unpublished materials in the field collections undertaken under the auspices of UNESCO. (p.111)

7.1.7 *Exploring the Intercultural Dimension of Music*

During the 18th Conference of ISME on the theme "A World View of Music Education" held in Canberra,

Australia from July 17 to 23, 1988, Kwabena Nketia presented a paper titled "Exploring Intercultural Dimensions of Music in Education" which was published in the ISME Yearbook 15 of the same year.

This paper echoes Nketia's recommendation of intercultural music education in his paper "New Perspectives in Music Education" presented a decade earlier. He begins the paper by stating categorically that the diversity that world music presents is an important challenge to the music educator, "for in music education the promotion of knowledge of diverse musical cultures has to be approached with intercultural understanding of music as a primary goal". (p.96). He then presents and discusses three major conceptual approaches to "how we can make sense of the diversity of world music" : 1) the relativist world view, 2) the comparative world view, and 3) the intercultural approach (pp. 96-101). According to him, of these three approaches:

> ...the intercultural approach which focuses on intercultural communication and understanding in music offers the greatest and most flexible scope for developing varied programmes in music education, for it can be applied to any set of musical cultures – those within one's own immediate environment, those with which one is frequently confronted by the media, the music of societies about whom one's pupils may have read or heard in their social studies lessons and so on". (p.101)

Nketia's exposé in the conclusion of this paper reflects the theme of the conference for which it was written. He emphasises that in this paper he has interpreted "a world view of music in education" as a call to music educators to make sense of the diversity of musical traditions that they encounter in their environment as well as those from other parts of the world (p.106). He adds that a world view of music education which makes intercultural understanding its primary objective, develops orientations which enable one to recognize similarities and assimilate or accommodate differences in musical traditions. Intercultural music education, Nketia believes, responds to "multiculturalism and the provision of national cultural policies intended to give due recognition to the music of minority cultures, but ensures that these are incorporated into a large educational objective which makes intercultural communication and understanding its primary goal". (p.106).

Nketia concludes this paper with the statement:

> ...a music educator must build bridges of knowledge and understanding not only between local traditions, but also between the musical cultures of the world, for if present trends are anything to go by, intercultural communication and understanding in music may become a dominant feature of the twenty-first century world of music (p.106)

He thus predicts the future of global music education in the new millennium.

7.2.1 A Summary of Nketia's Thoughts on Music Education

Nketia's thoughts on music education opined in his seven papers discussed in this chapter are summarised as follows:

Since music is an integral part of social life in African communities teachers should treat it as such in classrooms in Africa and stop giving undue prestige or importance to elements of foreign Western cultures.

The music of Africa – the music of the child's home and environment should be made the starting point of music education especially in primary schools in sub-Saharan Africa.

Music education should provide a link between the school and the community. The combination of the study of music education and ethnomusicology in music teacher education programmes will help bridge the gap between music in the classroom and music in the community.

Folk music should be used as a basis for the musical education of children. Music educators should have intimate knowledge of it. Folk music cannot be studied in isolation, hence the need for an interdisciplinary study of it with movement, language, arts and crafts, and drama.

Music educators must be aware of the social dimension to music education – the study of music in terms of the context of society and the context of culture. The socio-musical development of the child should, therefore, be the concern of music educators since this would ensure that the child developed a critical awareness of how music is practised in his/her society.

Music educators must make sense of the diversity of musical traditions that they encounter in their own environment as well as those from other parts of the world because it offers the greatest and most flexible scope for developing varied programmes in music education of all the musical cultures of the world.

7.2.2 A Critical Review of Nketia's Thoughts on Music Education

Did Kwabena Nketia's thoughts on music education expressed in the papers discussed in this chapter, change from time to time? In his two papers published in 1960 he proposed cultural music education based on the music of the child's society or environment. During the 1970s, as seen in his 1978 paper, he propagated intercultural music education based on what he describes as "philosophy of bi-musicality" (a combination of African and western musical cultures). It should be noted, however, that he had started nurturing this philosophy as far back as 1962 when he founded the School of Music, Dance and Drama (at the University of Ghana) which he described as "an experiment in bi-musicality". Thus the musical compositions he and other Ghanaian composers of the school wrote for its staff and students combined elements of both African and western music.

In Nketia's view, intercultural music education is the coroliary of multiculturalism which promotes the musical cultures of the world (see 1988 paper). He asserts that the intercultural approach to music education will result in an immense development of a diversity of world music programmes. It comes out clearly from his writings that the music of Africa (in the case of the African child) and the music of the child's home or environment (in the case of children from other parts of the world) should form the basis of music education especially in the primary school. Nketia, however, does not tell us at what stage of a person's formal education the intercultural music education should be started or emphasized. Should we assume that because he started intercultural music education (bi-musicality) at the university such an approach should be emphasized only at the tertiary level of education?

His prediction that intercultural music education may become a dominant feature of the twenty-first century global music education cannot be disputed. Indeed, multicultural music education is taking shape, although at a slow pace, in many countries of the world today.

The role Nketia expects the music teacher in Africa to play in the music education of the African child needs to be examined. Much as he concedes that music teachers in classrooms in Africa are handicapped in many areas, for example: lack of knowledge of indigenous African music; lack of understanding of African pedagogic principles; and lack of materials for teaching African music which hinder their ability to become successful teachers, Nketia, in this author's opinion, nevertheless expects too much from such teachers with regard to the music education of African school children. It seems to me that policy makers and curriculum experts in government departments or ministries of education should equally be expected to contribute positively to the development of school music education. Instances of new music syllabi not made available to music teachers or the lack of training of such teachers to teach the contents of such syllabi distributed to them have been with most sub-Saharan African countries since the post-colonial period of the 1960s. A music teacher in Africa, in such an environment, cannot give of his/her best and will be unable to, in Nketia's words, "treat music not as an object of instruction but as something vital, alive and part of experience" (see his first paper discussed in this chapter).

Nketia's suggestion that music educators study folk music not in isolation but combine it with the study of other disciplines like dance/movement, language, arts and crafts, and drama is problematic. An interdisciplinary approach to the study of the arts is a contentious issue many institutions of learning are not prepared or ready to deal with.

On the whole, Nketia's thoughts on music education are noble and they give us valuable information about the theory and practice of music education in Africa and the rest of the world.

CHAPTER EIGHT

THE PRACTICAL APPLICATION OF ETHNOMUSICOLOGY AND COMPOSITION IN THE PEDAGOGICAL PIECES AND EXERCISES IN AFRICAN RHYTHM

This chapter examines the practical application of Ethnomusicology and Composition in the pieces and exercises Nketia wrote in the 1960s to serve the needs of the School of Music, Dance and Drama (now School of Performing Arts). Of the compositions and exercises mentioned in chapter three (p.25) of this biographical study only three of the solo piano pieces, *Antubam* for cello and piano, (see appendix) and the *Preparatory Exercises in African Rhythm* will be discussed in this chapter.

8.1 African Pianism: Twelve Pedagogical Pieces

The four solo piano pieces mentioned in chapter three together with eight other piano pieces were published under the above title in 1994. According to Nketia (1994:iii), these pieces were designed "to give the African piano student being nurtured on simplified and original versions of Western piano repertoire something with African rhythmic and tonal flavour that may enrich his experience, shape his orientation, sense of timing and co-ordination of rhythmic and tonal events".

Nketia uses a variety of traditional and popular sources as the basis of the compositions and this is reflected in the titles of the pieces in this volume. He also gives instructions on how the pieces should be performed: "As in traditional African practice each piece can be repeated once or twice except where a definite closure is indicated by a retard. The pianist can also select a number of them and play them as a suite. A few of them such as the *Volta Fantasy* and *Meditation* can stand on their own as concert pieces." (iii)

A brief history of the term "African Pianism" is appropriate at this stage. The concept African Pianism was pioneered by the eminent Nigerian pianist, composer and ethnomusicologist, Akin Euba, who succeeded Nketia as Andrew W. Mellon Professor of Music at the University of Pittsburgh when the latter retired from that position in 1991.

In his introduction to the proceedings of an international symposium and festival held at the University of Pittsburgh in October 1999, on the theme "Towards an African Pianism", Euba writes :

> Western keyboard instruments were introduced to Africa by Christian missionaries (dating from the mid-nineteenth century in West Africa) and were thereafter disseminated through trade and other agents of culture contact,... Today, they are among the most common Western instruments in Africa and (in their electronic forms) have been widely adopted by pop musicians. (p.5)

In developing the theme on African Pianism, Euba

(1989:151) states that techniques used "in the performance of (African) xylophones, thumb pianos, plucked lutes, drum chimes ... and the polyrhythmic methods of African instrumental music in general would form a good basis for an African pianistic style". The ingredients of an African pianism include (a) thematic repetition (b) direct borrowings of thematic material (rhythmical and/or tonal) from African traditional sources (c) the use of rhythmical and/or tonal motifs which, although not borrowed from specific (identifiable) traditional sources, are based on traditional idioms (d) percussive treatment of the piano". (ibid. 152). He later added a fifth ingredient, "making the piano behave like African instruments" (1993:8).

Nketia, one of the African composers who endorsed the concept of African pianism provides further insight into the theory of an African pianism in the preface (p.iii) of his *African Pianism: Twelve Pedagogical Pieces:*

> African pianism refers to a style of piano music which derives its characteristic idiom from the procedures of African percussion music as exemplified in bell patterns, drumming, xylophone and mbira music. It may use simple or extended rhythmic motifs or the lyricism of traditional songs and even those of African popular music as the basis of its rhythmic phrases. It is open ended as far as the use of tonal materials is concerned except that it may draw on the modal and cadential

characteristics of traditional music. Its harmonic idiom may be tonal, atonal, consonant or dissonant in whole or in part, depending on the preferences of the composer, the mood or impressions he wishes to create or how he chooses to reinforce, heighten or soften the jaggedness of successive percussive attacks. In this respect the African composer does not have to tie himself down to any particular school of writing if his primary aim is to explore the potential of African rhythmic and tonal usages.

Let us see how the above ethnomusicological aspects of African music are applied in some of Nketia's piano pieces in this volume. *[see appendix pp 203 - 210 for their scores].*

8.1.1 Play Time

This is the first of the twelve pieces. It was composed around 1957. According to Euba (1999:28), the piece is "based on two sources: a popular dance song in Nzema, a language spoken in Ghana, and a song from Eseni Ogbo, a traditional music and dance type of the Ijaw of Nigeria. The popular song is the main focus of the work, while the traditional song provides a contrasting section, but with a final cadence that allows for the piece to be concluded with a repeat of the main section". Botthe popular dance song and the traditional music and dance type are presented in regular melodic phrases in the right hand (RH) part of the piano:

The popular dance song (melody), in the top part (bars 1-4) is repeated in the lower part (bars 5-8). Both phrases modulate to the key of A major (dominant) at their cadential points. The rhythmic figure ♪♪♩ (used in bar 1) plays an important role in this piece. It is used in bars 16 and 18 of the traditional dance song and it permeates the third section of the piece (bars 21-33).

Unlike the popular dance song (bars 1-8) the traditional dance song (bars 9-20) appears in the top part of the piano throughout:

Its first phrase (bars 9-12) is presented in sequence in the second phrase (bars 13-15) and the third phrase (bars 15-20) is marked by repetition (bars 16-18 and 18-20).

Nketia uses tonal harmony in this piece. The first section (bars 1-8) is in key D major but there is modulation to the dominant, A major (bars 3-4 and 7-8) at the cadential points where chordal progressions from the dominant thirteenth chord (bars 3 and 7) to the tonic (bars 4 and 8) occur. Seventh and ninth chords are used here and there and this section also employs four-part writing. There is a touch of B minor in bar 15 of the second section which is dominated by three-part writing. Harmony does not seem to be too important in the third section which is dominated by the rhythmic figures

The structure of this piece is as follows :-
A ‖:B:‖ C A B (without repeat)
Bars 1-8; bars 9-20; bars 21-33; bars 1-8; bars 9-20

It should be noted that the importance of the two African (Ghanaian and Nigerian) melodies (A and B) is reiterated in the structure of this piece. The piece shows a remarkable confirmation of African elements (melody and rhythm) and Western idioms (tonality, harmony and form).

8.1.2 At the Cross Roads

This piece, composed in 1961, is based on the Akan proverb which says that the traveller who asks for directions never misses the right turning when he comes to a crossroad. Commenting on this piece, Euba (1999 :28) writes:

> The melodic lines of this piece based on this proverb are in the form of questions that are restated in various forms throughout the piece but which are only partially answered by the supporting parts until we reach the final phase. Brief moments of tension and relaxation are created through contrasting and parallel pitch lines, changes in modality and rhythmic progressions.

The materials used in this piece especially melody and rhythm are original and not derived from any   particular traditional song or piece.

The rhythmic figure ♩♪♪ which first appears in bar 3 of the RH top piano part permeates the piece:

Another important rhythmic figure ♩. ♪ used in this piece first appears in the L H (bar 2). It is prominent in the second half of the piece especially from bars 28 – 37. These simple rhythmic motifs are characteristic of African music.

An interesting feature of the piece is tonality. Nketia applies the principle of modality to the heptatonic scale. He begins the piece in key C but then uses a flattened seventh (B flat) in bars 9, 13 and 25 as well as 48 and 50. This reminds us of his statement that "the flattened seventh, is frequent and well established in Akan vocal music" (see Nketia, *African Music in Ghana* p.35). Similarly, the use of the augmented fourth (F sharp) in bars 19, 20, 33, 42 and 43 draws our attention to his statement "The raised fourth is somewhat rare in Akan music, though it occurs, sometimes as characteristic of individual style (ibid)". The last three bars of the piece (51-53) suggest an ending in the dorian mode.

Although the melodic and rhythmic materials used in this piece are original , some of them, especially the melodic materials, nevertheless, show an influence of Akan vocal music.

8.1.3 Volta Fantasy

The Volta is the name of Ghana's largest river and the source of the country's hydroelectric power. The area around the river is known as the Volta Region, inhabited by communities including the Anlo-Ewe from whose music Nketia obtained the tonal and rhythmic elements for this composition, written in 1967.

This piece is the longest of the twelve pieces in this volume. It derives its basic rhythmic ideas from the bell pattern (time line) commonly associated with the Ewe dance agbadza as well as other Anlo-Ewe dances. This pattern notated on monotone

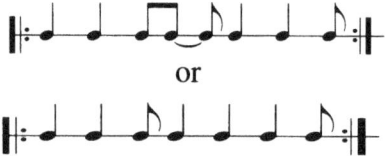

(see Nketia; *African Music in Ghana* p.85), is "presented in bold or naked form" (Agawu, 1999:4) mainly in the LH of the piano (bars 28-40)

The percussive presentation of this rhythmic pattern is made more effective with the RH joining the LH in its statement (bars 30 –31). Nketia skilfully uses variations in pitch to imitate the low and high pitches of the Anlo-Ewe double bell/gong, gankogui. In the above music quotation, the notes E (bars 28, 30 and 32) and F (bars 29 and 31) represent the sound of the lower bell while the other notes A and B in the passage represent the sound of the upper bell. Such is the importance of this rhythmic pattern that Agawu (ibid.) remarks that a performer unaware of its dance origins misses a crucial dimension of performance practice. In bars 83-95 the rhythmic pattern (first presented in bars 28-40) reappears not in bold or naked form", but with occasional fourths and fifths characteristic of the music of the Anlo-Ewe. The prevalent element in this piece is rhythm and Agawu, who grew up in the Volta

Region, aptly says, "For those who have grown up with the agbadza dance, hearing this rhythm in the Volta Fantasy is an invitation to dance, not of course actually but imaginatively." (Agawu, 1999:4)

The tonal organisation of this piece is based on various integrations and permutations of the hemitonic and anhemitonic pentatonic scales and the use of parallel octaves and occasional fourths and fifths – all common features in the music of the Anlo-Ewe. It should be noted that fourths and fifths appear in the RH part of the piano while parallel octaves are usually found in the LH part of the piano.

8.2   Antubam

Nketia inserts the word 'Epitaph' in brackets below the title of this elegiac piece for solo cello and piano which has several sections with contrasting tonalities, rhythms and colour. *[see appendix pp 210-214]*

Unlike his twelve pedagogical pieces, Nketia clearly indicates in alphabetical order the various sections of this piece in his score. *Antubam* is written in   time with a combination of duple and triple rhythms which is considered very important in African rhythmic procedure (see Nketia, *African Music in Ghana,* p. 79). Below is a section by section analysis of the piece:

Section A

This section is presented in twelve bars (1-12) consisting of three four-bar phrases. The piano and the cello are in dialogue in bars 1-8 but come together in bars 9-12. Three remarkable features of this section are the composer's use of : I) rhythm; 2) pitch; and 3) tonality.

Rhythm

In bars 1- 4 the piano rhythm ♩ ♪♫|♪♩ is immediately followed by the cello rhythm ♩. ♩ ♪|♩. In my opinion the piano rhythm may act as a bell/gong while the cello rhythm may be slated for a drum. After the contrasting piano rhythm in bars 5 and 6, ♫♩ ♫♩|♪ ♩ there is a return to the rhythm (used bars 1-4) in bars 7 and 8. The cello has a different rhythm ♪♩ ♩ ♪ in bar 8 and yet another rhythm ♪ ♩ which occurs from bars 9 through 12 where the piano also has new rhythms. Although the entire section A is replete with rests in both the piano and cello parts the two instruments are so rhythmically interlocked that the listener may be unaware of the occurrence of rests in the music.

Pitch

The piano part is dominated by unison melodic fragments which are an octave apart. Bar 12 consists of double thirds which are also an octave apart. According to Nketia (see *African Music in Ghana*, p.54) "singing in unison or in octaves, where men and women sing together, is a common form of choric organisation in Ghana, ...". Undoubtedly he tries to apply this ethnomusicological finding practically in this section of his composition.

The cello part employs repeated notes (E above middle C in bars 1 –8 but is dropped an octave lower in bars 9-11 and finally changes to A below middle C in bar 12). Intervals which are prevalent in this section are thirds and octaves. There are a few instances of falling fourths as well as rising or falling seconds.

Tonality

This section of the piece is in the Aeolian mode although the twelfth bar gives it a dorian effect.

Lastly the pizzicato (plucked) cello part in this section provides a beautiful contrast of sonority against the legato piano part.

Section B (bars 13-35 with a repeat)

This section is much longer, almost twice as long as Section A. The cello plays arco (with the bow) this time, a serene, lyrical, elegiac and modal melody mainly in its middle register. This melody has the characteristics of an African song, of course without a text, evident in its rhythms and tonality. It is a dirge.

The piano part, which is a contrast of section A, comprises chords (mainly in four parts as opposed to the linear harmony in Section A) and provides the harmony of this section. Another important feature of the piano part here is the use of parallel octaves in the LH (bars 27, 29, 34 and 35) at the low register of the instrument.

Section C (bars 36-56)

The cello has the melodic material in its high register as it plays in the treble clef throughout this section. It engages in a dialogue with the piano (bars 36-40) but the latter instrument virtually doubles its melody in the RH part (bars 41-44). Nketia applies Akan vocal music (melodic) techniques in his compositional process in this section. For example the use of the note B flat (a flattened seventh) in both the cello and piano parts, and the note F sharp (augmented fourth) in the piano part only, confirm his statement, "whereas a raised fourth is generally approached from the note above, the flattened seventh may be approached from a note above or below" (see Nketia, African Music in Ghana, p.35). There is also an application of African/Akan rhythm in the piano part (bars 46-48) where the instrument plays a combination of duple and triple rhythms.

    The composer exhibits remarkable skills with regard to the use of tonality in this section. Although the cello melody in the entire section seems to suggest the use of keys C and F, the accompanying piano part shows modulations (sometimes transient) to several keys: F minor in bars 37-38; G major in bars 40-43; G natural minor in bars 46-48; F major in bars 49-54 with a touch of D minor in bars 55-57. Nketia's use of modulations in this section cannot be said to be African, nevertheless, it is done with the combination of the aforementioned characteristics of Akan vocal music.

Section D

This is the shortest section of the piece. It consists of only four bars (57-60) in which the cello returns to the use of the bass clef as well as pizzicato as it did in section A. The most important element here is rhythm, presented in the cello part in bars 57 and 58 as ♪ ♩ ♪ and picked up by the piano L H in bar 59.

Section E (bars 61-72)

The cello returns to the use of the treble clef, an indication of the high register of its melodic material. Its melody in this section is agitated and this is reflected in its use of accented notes, repeated notes, and chromaticism. The rhythm of this part which combines duple and triple effects can be described as African. The piano part in this section is adventurous in terms of the use of tonality. Three 'unrelated' keys: A flat major (bars 62-64); D flat major (bars 65-70) and F sharp minor (bar 72) are used in this 12-bar section. The cello rhythm in section D, occasionally appears (though sometimes changed to ♪ ♩ ♩ 𝄽) in the piano part.

Section F (bars 73 –90)

The cello plays the same melody it played in Section C but this time, in the bass clef and in new keys beginning in A major and then passing through E major, back to A major, B minor (transient), back to A major and finally A minor in its last two bars. The "African" rhythm used in section C (bars 46-48) reappears here in bars 83-85 also in the piano part.

Section G (bars 91-102)

This is the exact return of section A

Section H (bars 103-130)

This is the exact return of section B except for the last six bars (125-130) which act as a coda and in which the key of C major is firmly established.

The fact that *Antubam* is concluded with a repeat of its first 35 bars containing the serene introduction and the lyrical and elegiac cello melody shows that sections A and B are the main focus of this piece. They constitute the dirge. Nketia (cv, p.17) describes this piece as a "dirge for cello and piano".

8.3 Preparatory Exercises in African Rhythm

As mentioned in chapter three (p.41) of this biographical study this booklet was produced for the study and practice of students to help them master the African rhythmic and melodic patterns used in Nketia's compositions.

Nketia says in the introduction to this booklet that it has been designed "for those already acquainted with the staff notation who wish to acquire proficiency in reading "African rhythm".

The booklet begins with simple rhythms, first presented in bare form and on monotone, and then there are exercises such as those used in children's songs after which we are introduced to new features of rhythm we are likely to encounter in simple Ghanaian traditional music. Furthermore, traditional and popular Ghanaian songs embodying particular rhythmic features dealt with in the exercises are provided for our study. They have been selected from different Ghanaian languages (such as Akan (Twi), Ga, Adangme, Sisala, Kasem and Builsa) but only the tunes are given so that the reader is not confronted with an additional problem of learning the texts.

Nketia advises that in learning the exercises and the songs, the reader must maintain a steady beat and where necessary reinforce it with some sort of regular bodily movement, stamping of the foot or handclapping – all characteristics of traditional Ghanaian musical practice. The development of a "metronome sense" by the reader is essential and Nketia points out that it will enable the reader to "maintain a steady basic beat mentally when complex rhythms have to be sung or played".(p.2). To enable the reader to acquire this steady beat: 1) the bar line has been used for marking the position of the regulative beat, and 2) metronome markings are indicated for each of the traditional and popular songs.

For those interested in following up the exercises and songs in this booklet, the author refers them to his earlier writings notably *African Music in Ghana* and *Folk Songs of Ghana*. Indeed, similar exercises in triple and duple measures and a combination of these rhythms, a common characteristic of Ghanaian music, are provided in the latter publication (p.11-15).

Nketia also says in his introduction to this booklet that the exercises may be sung or played on an appropriate musical instrument. Students who study voice or instruments like the atenteben, violin, flute will find them useful. These exercises and songs may be used for sight reading or sight singing to improve the reading skills of students in African rhythm.

Some of the pieces in this booklet may be played either on the piano or by two or three instruments. They are : No.11, *Kɛ lo aba wɔye* (Ga) written in two parts; No. 19 *Ashiele* (Ga) also written in two parts; and No.20 *Woma fai* (Ga) which begins with two-part writing in its opening four bars but changes to three-part writing from its fifth to its closing sixteenth bar.

Although Nketia's *Preparatory Exercises in African*

Rhythm was written almost four decades ago, it still has a great impact on the ethnomusicological literature on African rhythm. Much as Agawu agrees with this viewpoint he laments that Nketia's work as well as the work of other scholars on African rhythm have not received the international recognition they deserve:

> Despite the extensive attention given to rhythm in the ethnomusicological literature, we still do not have a comprehensive thesaurus of musical-rhythmic figures that might be used for pedagogical purposes on an international basis. (Agawu, 1999:3)

Concluding Remarks

It should be noted that Kwabena Nketia and Akin Euba are the leading exponents of the contentious concept 'African Pianism.' Indeed, the concept has been critized by some scholars' especially Agawu (1999) and Lucia (2000) who have written polemical papers on it. This writer has tried in this chapter to help the reader discover some of the characteristics of 'African Pianism' in Nketia's work. He does, not, therefore, argue in favour or against the concept 'African Pianism'.

CHAPTER NINE

NKETIA'S LEGACY

Chapters one through eight of this biographical study have dealt with Kwabena Nketia's ability to share the knowledge and experience he acquired from his research and writings over the past five decades, especially with his students and fellow scholars, and generally with music educators, artists and music lovers.

This short, last chapter is devoted to what he leaves for us to maintain or improve on where necessary. His legacy will be discussed in four areas in which he excells, namely musical composition, research in African music and culture, music education and Akan (Twi) literature.

Musical Composition

As mentioned in chapters one and three, Nketia wrote many songs and choral pieces, with Twi texts, which are well-known in Ghana. His choral compositions are often included in the repertoire of many choirs in Ghana. Indeed, his songs and choral works have made such an impact on Ghanaians that Akrofi (1992:41) remarked that: "Ghanaians know him best as a composer and associate his name with his song, 'Yaanom Montie' and his choral compositions for unaccompanied SATB choirs - "Monkamfo No",

"Nkyirimma Nyɛ Bi" and "Monna N'ase."

Ephraim Amu and Kwabena Nketia are the most revered composers of choral music in Ghana. But Nketia made further contributions than Amu to instrumental music composition. His pedagogical pieces for the piano and other instrumental pieces, originally written for the staff and students of the School of Music, Dance and Drama in the 1960s and 1970s, continue to be included in the repertoire of present generation of music students and professional artists especially in Ghana and the U.S.A., where he has lived and worked most of his life.

Research in African Music and Culture

Nketia's field research output not only paved the way for the study of ethnomusicology at the University of Ghana but has also made the institution one of the world's centres for the study of African music and dance. His initiative led to the establishment of three institutions on the campus of the University of Ghana, namely the Institute of African Studies, School of Performing Arts, and International Centre for African Music and Dance, all of which are striving to continue with the work started by him.

The Ghana Dance Ensemble, which Nketia and Opoku founded four decades ago and the Hewale Sounds, formed only four years ago, continue to tour Ghana and other parts of the world to promote African music and dance. Most of Nketia's colleagues with whom he started his programme at the University of

Ghana have either died or retired. With Nketia's imminent retirement, the younger generation of Ghanaian scholars, many of whom are working abroad, should team up and continue from where he left off. Internationally, Kwabena Nketia has been regarded as the most prominent scholar in the field of African music, who readily shared his experience of such music with fellow scholars. In a tribute to Nketia, Posnansky (as quoted in Carter, 1990:3) described him as "the first African musicologist to make a significant impact on a discipline previously dominated by Europeans and South Africans". We should also recall Agawu's (2000:1) tribute to Nketia: "How much the field would be without his contributions" (in chapter five of this study).

Music Education

Nketia has always fought for the inclusion of African music in the music curricula of schools in Africa, which are still either dominated by or exclusively devoted to Western art music. This should encourage the present generation of Ghanaians and other Africans to ensure that their indigenous music is not suppressed by the music of other cultures within or outside their school systems.

Although the African pedagogical principles Nketia proposed for African music instruction in schools have been elusive, he nevertheless, has made African music educators aware of the need to give some recognition to the study of African music in such institutions. Nketia's *Preparatory Exercises in African Rhythm,* his pedagogical work designed to acquaint students, teachers and music lovers with rhythm, the sine qua non of African music, still has a great impact on the ethnomusicological literature on African rhythm. The present generation of African scholars must continue the much needed work in African rhythm in order to give it the unique character it has in African music even in this era of globalisation.

Akan Literature

As mentioned in chapter three of this study, Nketia has made a significant contribution to the development of Akan literature with his writings in Twi. Twi is also the language he uses in his songs and choral works and his excellent knowledge of it helped him to understand and collect Akan song texts during his fieldwork. His publications on two noble but dying indigenous Akan professions of hunting and drumming resulting from his collection of the text of the Akan hunters' songs and Akan drum language played on the atumpan, are an attempt to preserve, promote and develop Akan culture which the present generation of Ghanaians should emulate. His other Twi works like anthologies of folktales, plays and poems are valuable materials for the study of Akan language and literature in Ghanaian educational institutions.

Finally, we should be proud of the outstanding work of Kwabena Nketia, a scholar and music educator of such rare distinction.

Notes

1. *"Sika-rebewu- ɛpere* was a popular traditional Akan dance in the 1920s. Nketia (see *Drumming in Akan Communities of Ghana* p.70) cites it as one of the popular dances superseded by new ones. He adds that with the exception of Adowa, many Akan popular dances enjoyed a short life of some four or five years, after which they began to wane, dissolve or change as new ones began to gain a footing.

2. *"Sukuu"* is the Twi word for school. *"Sukuu mu"* literally means an area where a school is located.

3,4 These are Akan traditional musical types. *Adowa* is performed by a mixed group of men and women while *nnwonkorɔ* is a female only musical type.

5. The Akan who constitute about 60% of Ghana's population comprise of ethnic groups of people such as Asante, Akim, Brong, Fante and Kwawu who live in the Southern part of the country.

6. Smallwood's Pianoforte Tutor was a keyboard learning book used in those days for teaching the piano. It is still used by keyboard teachers and students.

7. Stewart Macpherson was a British author whose books on harmony and theory of music were used as textbooks in Ghana between the 1920s and 1970s.

8. Highlife – a Ghanaian popular musical form which dates back to the 1920s. The term was created by people who gathered around dance clubs to watch and listen to couples enjoying themselves. The people outside called it "highlife" as they could not match the class of the people in such clubs.

9. Dondology is derived from the Twi word *'dondo'* – name for the hourglass drum.

10. Between 1964 and 1966, the author, who was a student at Achimota School, about 5km from the campus of the University of Ghana, received free cello tuition from Judith and was inspired to study the instrument at the Royal Academy of Music, London, between 1968 and 1972.

11. The 1975 meeting, one of earliest of the General Assembly, was held on the premises of the Ghana Broadcasting Corporation in Accra, Ghana. The organisers of the meeting included the late father of the author, Mr George E. Akrofi, who was then Director of Music and Culture at the Ghana Broadcasting Corporation.

12. After Professor Nketia retired from the University of Ghana in 1979, the School of Music, Dance and Drama was renamed School of Performing Arts and was first headed by Professor Joe de Graft, a renowned Ghanaian writer.

13. The author taught Kofi Agawu music at Achimota School in 1972 when the latter was a Sixth Form student.

14. We learn from the Introduction of this book that this musical form was in ancient times performed by women whose husbands and sons were away on the battlefield to ask God's grace for the safe return of their relatives. According to Nketia, these texts are short, sung in a rhythm imitating that of ordinary speech, and sometimes replete with repetition. Examples are No. 94-105. (95, 97, 98 and 99 are very short).

BIBLIOGRAPHY

Agawu, V. Kofi. 1995 *African Rhythm : A Northern Ewe Perspective.* Cambridge : Cambridge University Press.

_____. 1999 "Is African Pianism Possible?". Paper delivered at the Symposium and Festival, "African Pianism," University of Pittsburgh, October 1999.

_____. 2000 "The Legacy of Ephraim Amu", Paper delivered for The Ephraim Amu Memorial Lecture at the National Theatre, Accra on Tuesday, January 18th, 2000.

Akrofi, Eric A. 1982 "The Status of Music Education Programs in Ghanaian Public Schools" Ed.D. dissertation, University of Illinois at Urbana –Champaign.

_____. 1992 "Personalities in World Music Education No.14– J.H. Kwabena Nketia", *International Journal of Music Education* No.19, pp. 41- 45

Carter, William G. 1990 Foreword, *African Musicology: Current Trends* Volume II. Los Angeles : University of California, African Studies Center.

Cohen, Marilyn and Addo, Jasper. Eds. 1998 *ICAMD Newsletter,* Legon: International Centre for African

Music and Dance, University Of Ghana No.2, September.

DjeDje, J.C. and Carter, W.G. eds. 1989 *African Musicology : Current Trends*, Los Angeles : African Studies Center and African Arts Magazine, University of California

Euba, Akin, 1989 *Essays on Music in Africa 2: Intercultural Perspective.* Bayreuth : Bayreuth African Studies.

_____. 1993 *Modern African Music: A Catalogue of Selected Archival Material at Iwalewa-Haus, University of Bayreuth, Germany.* Bayreuth: Iwalewa-Haus.

_____. 1999 ed. *Towards an African Pianism: Keyboard Music of Africa and Its Diaspora.* Program and Notes of Symposium and Festival 7-9 October. University of Pittsburgh.

Fiagbedzi, Nissio, 1990 *"Toward a Philosophy of Theory in Ethnomusicological Research."* African Musicology: Current Trends Vol. 1 Los Angeles: African Studies Centre and African Arts Magazine, University of Carfornia p.45 - 55

Jones, A.M. 1962 "Book Review of *African Music in Ghana* by J.H. Kwabena Nketia". *African Music Society Journal* 3(i) : 116

LeComte, Richard. 1992 "Fusing rhythms of the past, present." *Lawrence: Journal World,* Friday Jan. 31 p 48

Lucia Christine, 2000 *"Towards an African Pianism": Piano Music of Africa and the Diaspora, Symposium and Festival"* South African Journal of Musicology Vol. 19/20 pp 131-135

Ndlovu, Caesar and Akrofi, Eric. 1999 "The State of Research in the Performing Arts of South Africa". *Bulletin: Issues in the Human Sciences.* Vol.6 No.1 October. Pretoria : National Research Foundation, p. 14-15

_____. 1949 *Akanfoɔ Nnwom Bi.* London : Oxford University Press.

_____. 1955 *Funeral Dirges of the Akan People.* Achimota.

_____. 1962 *African Music in Ghana.* London: Longmans Green and Co.

_____. 1962 "The Problem of Meaning in African Music" *Ethnomusicology: Journal of the Society for Ethnomusicology* 6 (i) : 1-7, January.

_____. 1963 *Drumming in Akan Communities of Ghana.* Edinburgh and London: University of Ghana and Thomas Nelson and Sons, Ltd.

_____. 1963 *Folk Songs of Ghana.* London: Oxford University Press

_____. 1963 *Preparatory Exercises in African Rhythm.* Legon : Institute of African Studies, School of Music and Drama, University of Ghana.

_____. 1965 *Music, Dance and Drama : A Review of the Performing Arts of Ghana.* Accra-Tema : Ghana Information Services.

_____. 1966 "Music Education in African Schools : *A Review of the Position in Ghana, "International Seminar on Teacher Education in Music, Proceedings,* pp. 231-243

_____. 1967 "The Place of Authentic Folk Music in Education", *Music Educators Journal* 54 (3) : 40-42, 129-133, November.

_____. 1968 Our *Drums and Drummers.* Accra : Ghana Publishing House.

_____. 1970a Ethnomusicology in Ghana : An Inaugural Lecture delivered on 20th November 1969 at the University of Ghana, Legon. Accra : Ghana Universities Press

_____. 1970b "Music Education in Africa and the West : We Can Learn From Each Other", *Music Educators Journal* 57 (3) : 48-55 November.

_____. 1971 "The Objectives of Music Education in Contemporary Africa." Paper read at the Lusaka Music Conference, June 15-22, Legon : Institute of African Studies.

_____. 1974 *The Music of Africa*. New York : W.W. Norton and Co., Inc

_____. Ed. 1975 N*otes on Education and Research in African Music*. No.2 July

_____. 1978 "New Perspectives in Music Education" *International Music Education. ISME Yearbook*. V:104-111

_____. 1981 "The Juncture of the Social and the Musical : The Methodology of Cultural Analysis", *The World of Music* 23 (2) : 22-35

_____. 1984 "The Aesthetic Dimension in Ethnomusicological Studies," *The World of Music* 26 (1):3-28

_____. 1986 "African Music and Western Praxis : A Review of Western Perspectives on African Musicology", *Canadian Journal of African Studies* 20(i) :36-56

_____. 1988 "Exploring Intercultural Dimensions of Music in Education" International Music Education. *ISME Yearbook XV*: 96-106

_____. 1963 *Folk Songs of Ghana*. London: Oxford University Press

_____. 1963 *Preparatory Exercises in African Rhythm*. Legon : Institute of African Studies, School of Music and Drama, University of Ghana.

_____. 1965 *Music, Dance and Drama : A Review of the Performing Arts of Ghana*. Accra-Tema : Ghana Information Services.

_____. 1966 "Music Education in African Schools : *A Review of the Position in Ghana, "International Seminar on Teacher Education in Music, Proceedings,* pp. 231-243

_____. 1967 "The Place of Authentic Folk Music in Education", *Music Educators Journal* 54 (3) : 40-42, 129-133, November.

_____. 1968 Our *Drums and Drummers*. Accra : Ghana Publishing House.

_____. 1970a Ethnomusicology in Ghana : An Inaugural Lecture delivered on 20th November 1969 at the University of Ghana, Legon. Accra : Ghana Universities Press

_____. 1970b "Music Education in Africa and the West : We Can Learn From Each Other", *Music Educators Journal* 57 (3) : 48-55 November.

_____. 1971 "The Objectives of Music Education in Contemporary Africa." Paper read at the Lusaka Music Conference, June 15-22, Legon : Institute of African Studies.

_____. 1974 *The Music of Africa*. New York : W.W. Norton and Co., Inc

_____. Ed. 1975 N*otes on Education and Research in African Music*. No.2 July

_____. 1978 "New Perspectives in Music Education" *International Music Education. ISME Yearbook*. V:104-111

_____. 1981 "The Juncture of the Social and the Musical : The Methodology of Cultural Analysis", *The World of Music* 23 (2) : 22-35

_____. 1984 "The Aesthetic Dimension in Ethnomusicological Studies," *The World of Music* 26 (1):3-28

_____. 1986 "African Music and Western Praxis : A Review of Western Perspectives on African Musicology", *Canadian Journal of African Studies* 20(i) :36-56

_____. 1988 "Exploring Intercultural Dimensions of Music in Education" International Music Education. *ISME Yearbook XV*: 96-106

_____. 1990 "Contextual Strategies of Inquiry and Systematization" Charles Seeger Memorial Lecture. *Ethnomusicology* 34 (i): 75-97

_____. 1991 "Music and Cultural Policy in Contemporary Africa" *Music in the Dialogue of Cultures: Traditional Music and Cultural Policy* edited by Max Peter Bauman. Wilhelmshaven, Florian Noetzel Verlag 77-94.

_____. 1994 *African Pianism : Twelve Pedagogical Pieces.* Published for International Centre of African Music and Dance by Afram Publications (Ghana) Limited.

_____. 1995 "National Development and the Performing Arts of Africa". International Centre for African Music and Dance

_____. n.d. "The Challenge of Cultural Preservation in a Dynamic Social Environment". Paper read at the National Festival Of Arts NAFAC '98 Symposium. International Centre for African Music and Dance.

_____. n.d. "Intellectual Agenda for Coping with Social Reality" Presidential Address, 38th Anniversary of the Ghana Academy of Arts and Sciences.

Tracey, Hugh. 1956 "Book Review of Funeral Dirges of the Akan People By J.H. Nketia" *African Music Society Journal* 1 (3) : 82

Vieta, Kojo T. 1999 *The Flagbearers of Ghana: Profiles of One Hundred Distinguished Ghanaians.* Volume 1 Accra : Ena Publications pp. 445-450.

APPENDIX

PLAY TIME

AT THE CROSS ROAD

VOLTA FANTASY

ANTUBAM

www.ingramcontent.com/pod-product-compliance
Lightning Source LLC
Chambersburg PA
CBHW071354290426
44108CB00014B/1543